Shackleton
at War and Peace

Shackleton
at War and Peace

ROYAL AIR FORCE

120

John Chartres

LONDON
IAN ALLAN LTD

First published 1989

ISBN 0 7110 1838 3

© John Chartres 1989

Published by Ian Allan Ltd, Shepperton,
Surrey; and printed by Ian Allan Printing Ltd at
their works at Coombelands in Runnymede,
England

Half title:
MR3 XF708 photographed at Duxford in June 1988. *Alan Curry*

Previous page:
MR3 WR981 of No 120 Squadron. *BAe*

Below:
AEW2s of No 8 Squadron. *RAF Official*

Below right:
Mk 3 of No 201 Squadron as seen by the pilot of another one over Singapore in 1967.
Wg Cdr R. K. Page RAAF (Retd)

Contents

Acknowledgements

My first thanks must go to all those who responded so generously to my appeals for information with words and pictures, and to the editors of such publications as *RAF News*, *Air Mail* (the newsletter of the Royal Air Forces Association), *Air Clues* and the newsletter of the recently formed Shackleton Association who printed them.

Mr John Botwood, the founder of the latter organisation and editor of the first issues of its newsletter, now called *The Growler*, has also made a noteworthy contribution to the text. I have to thank the editor of *Air Clues* a second time for permission to reproduce John Botwood's account of Shackleton life in the 1950s.

For recent information on the operations of the last six Shackletons I would like to thank many members of No 8 Squadron RAF, particularly its OC, Wg Cdr David Hencken; his Senior Engineering Officer, Sqn Ldr Mike Duiguid; Flt Lts Andy Thomas and Rupert Hornby; WO Peter Heap and CTech Paul Emery.

I have had the most valuable help from the restoration team which has worked, and still is working, on WR960 in the Air & Space Gallery of the Greater Manchester Museum of Science and Technology, especially from its leader Mr Dennis Stead and from Mr Michael McCabe, the compiler of many statistics on Shackletons. Dr Alan Curry of Manchester has been particularly generous in the loan of many photographs as have been Mr Peter R. March and several other professional aviation photographers.

Mr Gordon Swanborough, editor of *Air Enthusiast*, has given me permission to draw on a long article which I wrote myself by arrangement with Ian Allan Ltd, especially the table of fatal accidents. Again 'Aircraft Profile' No 243 by Mr Peter J. Howard has proved a most valuable cross-check. Details of the 'Ballykelly Railway' first appeared in *Fly Past*.

Mr Robert Symons and Mr Louis Vosloo have provided me with important updating on the fate of the now grounded SAAF Mk 3s.

I found ACM Sir David Lees's book *Flight from the Middle East* a most valuable reference for the section on Shackleton operations in that theatre of war.

Air Cdre Henry Probert RAF (Retd) and Gp Capt T. C. Flanagan MSc, BA (Hons) RAF (Retd), gave me much help in the compilation of my earlier book *Avro Shackleton* as did Mr Harry Holmes of British Aerospace, Woodford, and aviation historians Brian Robinson of Stockport and James D. Ferguson of Aberdeen. I would like to thank them again.

Wherever possible I have endeavoured to attribute photographs and sketches to those who took or drew them, but with the passage of time this has not always been possible. I have, however, recently discovered that a number of cartoons which first appeared in *Coastal Through the Looking Glass* were the work of George Heald, a signaller on No 120 Squadron, whose name should certainly be on record!

Author's Preface

When it became clear to me and to my publishers that the Shackleton was about to break all world records for longevity we were faced with a problem. My previous book *Avro Shackleton* in the Ian Allan 'Postwar Military Aircraft' series had sold out. Should we, therefore, update it and produce a second edition in time for the 40th anniversary of the type's first flight due on 9 March 1989? Or should we try to produce a completely new book to mark this occasion? The decision made by Ian Allan Ltd was that we should try for the latter option. The publishers also decided that the next book should conform to their noted 'At War' series.

The other problem facing me as the author was how much repetition would be permissible from *Avro Shackleton*? During the research work into this book I discussed this matter with many people; past and serving members of the RAF associated with the Shackleton and young people very much concerned with the recording of aviation history. All agreed that this should be a complete book in its own right and that therefore some repetition of both facts and pictures from *Avro Shackleton* would not only be acceptable, but indeed desirable.

So it has turned out. Perhaps like so many solutions to problems it may be a compromise. I have endeavoured to put in as much new material as possible, especially in the form of the personal reminiscences I have gleaned, much from those mentioned in the Acknowledgements section, and of course some new information about how the last six Shackletons operated by No 8 Squadron at Lossiemouth are being kept in the sky until the probable 'end-date', some time in 1991, information obtained from members of 8 Squadron.

If, as it seems, the final operational sortie by a Shackleton takes place around that time, then this aeroplane design will really have become a world-beater in terms of longevity.

John Chartres
Hale, Cheshire
1989

6

The Concept and Evolution of the Shackleton

SHACKLETON G.R. MK I

Above:
The first sketch of a Shackleton. *British Aerospace (BAe)*

Overleaf:
'Long in memory, but not short in wind' (with apologies to Edward Bowen, writer of the words of the Harrow football song) — an atmospheric study of a Shackleton photographed off the Scottish coast. *Allan Richardson Collection*
(Author's Note: Several attempts have been made to trace the origin of this outstanding photograph without success!)

Writers and historians learn at an early stage of their careers to be wary of superlatives. In the case of Type 696, better known as the Avro Shackleton, the general claim is that by 1989, the year of publication of this book, it will have flown for 40 years from the date of the first flight at Woodford on 9 March 1949. All the indications are that the type will achieve 40 years of frontline RAF operational service by 1991, the current 'end-date' for the last operations with Shackleton AEW2s by No 8 Squadron at Lossiemouth.

In laying claim for a probable world longevity record the phrase 'frontline operational service' is used advisedly to rule out such contenders as the DC-3/C-47 Dakota design and even the DH89 Rapide/Dominie and perhaps some others.

On the longevity claim, however, one does have to be careful about the Canberra. The English Electric Canberra first flew on 13 May 1949, just over two months after the late Mr Jimmy Orrell's take-off in Shackleton prototype WV126 at Woodford on 9 March. The first Canberras entered RAF service in May 1951 in No 101 Squadron at Binbrook. The first Shackletons entered service with No 120 Squadron at Kinloss in March that year. It is therefore a close-run thing when claiming such longevity records.

In this author's submission the Shackleton wins over the Canberra on two grounds. One is that the Canberra was, in

design, ahead of its time as Britain's first jet bomber, whereas in all fairness the Roy Chadwick Shackleton 'shape' could really be traced back to the Manchester of 1938-39, its lineage then going through the Lancaster, the Lincoln and the Tudor perhaps conferring on it 50 years of longevity. Although some 50 Canberras were still in RAF and Fleet Air Arm (FAA) service at the time of writing and perhaps several hundred still flying in various parts of the world it remained questionable whether any deserved the title of 'frontline operational service'. Those closest to this category would probably be the aircraft flown on somewhat mysterious Electronic Counter-Countermeasures (ECM) operations from RAF Wyton about which journalists and historians are not really encouraged to write in much detail.

Above:
An English Electric Canberra, exemplified here by T4 WE195 in about 1967. *Alan Curry*

Below:
Canberra TT18 WK124 of No 100 Squadron, seen at RAF Waddington in 1988. *Alan Curry*

Above right:
One of the last flying Short Sunderlands, Mk V ML824 in French markings, being escorted to Britain by Shackletons of No 201 Squadron before being put on display at Hendon. *MoD*

Right:
The last operational RAF Lancaster, MR3 RF325, going out of service at St Eval in October 1956.

Above:
An Avro Lincoln.

Above right:
An early line drawing of the Lincoln profile. *BAe*

Centre right:
Early line drawing of the Shackleton Mk 1 profile. *BAe (Note: these drawings are NOT to the same scale.)*

Right:
Always a comforting sight. *Rolls-Royce*

For better or for worse, then, this book claims that the Shackleton is a world record holder in terms of longevity under that label of frontline operational service. Arguments may continue to rage over this assertion and they will be followed with interest by this author and his publishers.

To begin at the beginning then the requirement for the Shackleton under Air Ministry Specification R5/46 issued on 17 March 1947 came about because Coastal Command needed a new long-range land-based aeroplane to carry out its postwar commitments. Soon after the end of World War 2 'Coastal', which had to return its mainstay landplane fleet of Liberators and Fortresses to the United States at the conclusion of the Lease-Lend arrangement, could not proceed any further with flying boat development and was left with a small force of Lancasters in the Mk 3 General Reconnaissance (GR) and Mk 3 Air Sea Rescue (ASR) versions. Some Sunderlands remained in service, but for a lot of reasons which are not always fully understood, flying boat development was really at an end. Those who mourn the end of flying boat development perhaps do not always appreciate that this apparently omnifarious form of aeroplane always had its limitations; not being able to alight on or take-off from unsheltered water in safety, always being slower and more fuel-consuming than landplanes of the same size, and with its main *raison d'être* being removed by the existence of long runways in most parts of the world.

In the late 1940s Coastal Command's requirements were growing with the creation of NATO (the 'A' for 'Atlantic' in the title being especially significant) so

were those of the Middle and Far East Air Forces. There was, therefore, an urgent demand for a better VLR (Very Long Range) landplane than the Lancaster which, in all fairness, was a very good bomber but never really intended by its designer to be much more than just that. A larger, longer range and importantly a more comfortable aircraft was therefore urgently needed for both Coastal Command and for the Middle and Far East Air Forces. The question of comfort was not one of molly-coddling peacetime aircrews but one of sheer efficiency if they were to carry out missions lasting up to 20hr and remain capable of doing their jobs properly.

The first proposal from Avro, the obvious No 1 contender for the contract, was for an updated version of the Lincoln, itself really a hyped-up Lancaster originally planned for the conventional bombing of Japan if that had become necessary; and the description 'Lincoln 3' was at one stage used for what was later labelled Type 696 and then 'Shackleton'. (The name was in fact chosen by Roy Chadwick personally, partly because of his wife's relationship to the family of the great explorer, partly

because he thought it was entirely appropriate for an aeroplane which was going to range over long distances, often in hostile climatic conditions.)

There was never much doubt in anybody's mind that it would be A. V. Roe of Manchester which would come up with the right answer to Specification R5/46. Apart from anything else the company had the makings of the required design in the form of wing and tailplane assemblies from the Lincoln and from the Tudor, its ill-starred attempt to produce a postwar long range civil airliner — in one of which Roy Chadwick himself was tragically killed before he saw the first Shackleton fly. Another factor in the creation of the Shackleton was the availability of the potent Rolls-Royce Griffon 57 and 57A engines, developments of the Merlin, capable of delivering 2,500hp-plus through contra-rotating double airscrews.

Old-hand designers and engineers at the Avro, later Hawker Siddeley and finally British Aerospace factories at Chadderton and Woodford, tend to recall that the creation of the Shackleton was a relatively easy task. It was really a case of making a Lancaster or a Lincoln fuselage fatter all

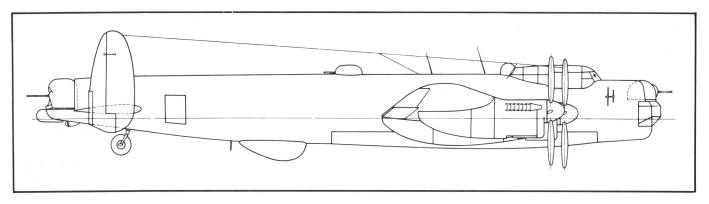

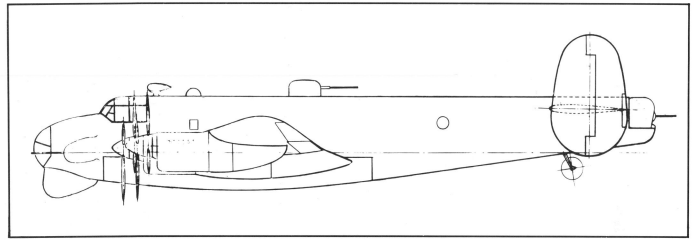

round, not only to accommodate more equipment but in particular to give aircrews reasonable space in which to move around during very long sorties; in which to keep themselves warm, and perhaps very importantly fill themselves from time to time with hot food and drink.

Roy Chadwick had, by the late 1940s, been elevated to the post of Technical Director of A. V. Roe from that of Chief Designer. This did not mean that he ceased to keep a personal eye on what was happening 'on the boards'. The Shackleton was after all going to be another of his 'shapes' and indeed his daughter, Mrs Margaret Dove, still remembers him coming home with its outline sketched in the margin of a copy of the *Manchester Evening News* which he had had in the train with him. As mentioned above, Roy Chadwick did not live to see the prototype Shackleton, the last of his 'shapes', take off on its first flight to commence its 40 years of service.

He died on 23 August 1947 while aboard the Avro Tudor II prototype which crashed on take-off for a routine test flight from

Woodford, along with Mr S. A. 'Bill' Thorn, the company's Chief Test Pilot; Sqn Ldr D. J. B. Wilson, chief of the flight test section, and Mr J. Webster, the radio operator. His death at the age of 54 was perhaps especially poignant for all concerned with the Shackleton. His daughter remembers clearly how the name of 'Shackleton' for Type 696 came about. Curiously, Roy Chadwick had at a much earlier stage in his career designed a little biplane seaplane, called the Avro Antarctic for Sir Ernest Shackleton's last expedition in the autumn of 1921.

In any appreciation of 'The Shackleton Shape' it should be remembered that Roy Chadwick designed the Manchester in response to the Air Staff Requirement of September 1936. This called for a twin-engined medium bomber to be powered by Rolls-Royce Vulture 24-cylinder engines.

Roy Chadwick designed the Manchester with this form of power supply, the only one open to him. The Vulture was probably one of the few bad engines ever designed or produced by Rolls-Royce and Roy Chadwick was never really happy

about the Manchester concept. His fears were justified when there were disastrous losses in the first raids carried out by Manchesters during World War 2, some of them attributable to engine failures, others to lack of power and speed when evasive tactics became necessary.

Roy Chadwick continued to press for a supply of Merlin engines in order to turn his 'shape' into an effective four-engined bomber.

At that stage (circa 1940) Merlin engines were 'rationed' — every single one desperately needed to replace the losses of Hurricanes and Spitfires during the Battle of Britain.

However, Roy Chadwick eventually persuaded Lord Beaverbrook and others to let him have some, and out of the deal emerged the Lancaster. Out of the Lancaster grew the Lincoln, plus such variants as the York — which apart from many other roles performed heroically during the Berlin Airlift — the Lancastrian, perhaps the very first British postwar airliner, and to some extent the rather ill-starred Tudor. Out of them all grew the Shackleton.

In essence then, VW126, the first prototype Shackleton, consisted of a much-fattened and deepened Lancaster/Lincoln fuselage; Lincoln/Tudor outer wing sections, and a strengthened and slightly reshaped Lincoln tail assembly. In what are now immortal words Mr J. H. Orrell ('Jimmy', who died in August 1988), Avro's Chief Test Pilot by 1949, with no fewer than 900 different Lancaster serial numbers in his logbook from his wartime days as a production test pilot, said about that first flight on 9 March 1949: 'It felt right. I knew it would feel right because it was a Roy Chadwick shape.'

Jimmy Orrell did one taxi-run and brought the aircraft back because he was unhappy about the amount of 'boot' he seemed to need on the rudders. He told the design staff that he could take the aircraft off and fly it but that he could not be answerable for what might happen if he, say, lost an engine or some other first test flight crisis arose, because of the rudder 'feel'.

He recalled that they all went to look at the fins and rudders and discovered that by some adjustments between trim and balance tabs the lateral control could be improved. He recalled that one Shackleton fin and rudder assembly had been put through wind tunnel tests at Coventry but that the readings obtained may not have properly assessed the performance of two such assemblies in unison; the effects of the rather curious slipstream brought about by the contra-rotating propellers were of course something new in multi-engined aircraft at that stage.

The adjustments only took an hour or so and Jimmy then took VW126 off for a 35min circuit of Woodford with Mr S. E. Esler as co-pilot, and Mr A. Blake as flight engineer. Shortly before he died at the age of 84 Jimmy Orrell told me that from that moment he knew the Shackleton was going to be a very good aeroplane, but at the time he did not really envisage it remaining in operational service for 40 years! He had hoped that he would be fit and well enough to perhaps 'hold the spectacles' during whatever 40th anniversary celebrations took place in March 1989, if invited to do so, but to the sadness of many in the Shackleton world this was not to be.

Above:
Mr J. H. 'Jimmy' Orrell photographed in about 1960. Mr Orrell died in August 1988. *BAe*

Below:
Running up VW126 before the first take-off on 9 March 1949; 'Jimmy' Orrell is at the controls. *BAe*

Above:
Airborne after a 14sec run. *BAe*

Below:
The second prototype — VW131. *BAe*

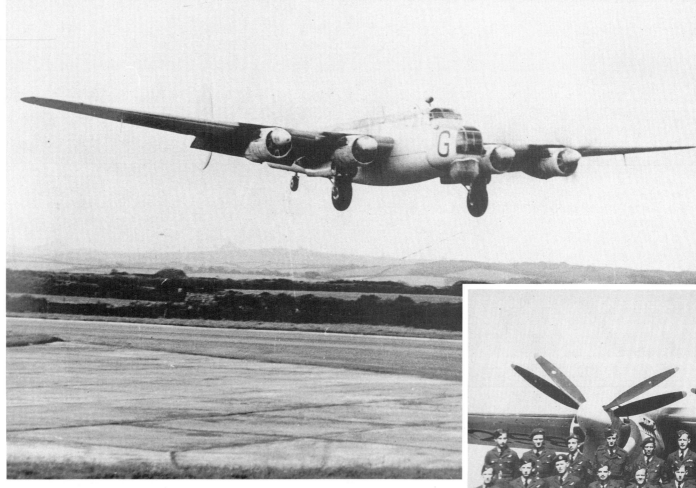

Top:
A Farnborough spectacular: demonstrations included low passes with three engines feathered and take-offs one day with a return the next. *RAF*

Above:
An early Mk 1 landing at Woodford. *BAe*

Right:
No 120 Squadron during the Intensive Flying/Acceptance Trials in 1951.
Allan Richardson collection

18

After the application of a few more pieces of fabric and glue on the rudders he made another 45min flight. The first prototype, VW126 was very much a 'one-off' aeroplane, being fitted among other things with two 20mm Hispano cannon in 'barbettes' on each side of the nose; two more in a Bristol B17 dorsal turret, and provision made for 0.5in machine guns in a tail turret. Rather significantly an in-flight refuelling point was located under the tail, designed to use an early system prepared for the Lancasters and Lincolns which might have been used for the conventional bombing of Japan if the atom bombs had not been dropped. No production Shackletons were ever equipped for in-flight refuelling. This would have been difficult under the system eventually adopted by the RAF using the drogue and probe arrangement, but one might ponder on whether some ship losses in the Falklands War might have been averted if some AEW Shackletons could have been flown out there with in-flight refuelling capability. Several of these features were omitted from the second and third prototypes (VW131 and VW135) although the dorsal gun turret was retained on the Mk 1 production aircraft and on some Mk 2s.

The first of the production MR1 (Maritime Reconnaissance) were delivered to the RAF at the turn of 1950-51, the earliest operational aircraft going to No 120 Squadron at Kinloss in March 1951 for acceptance trials. Others went at an early stage to No 224 Squadron at Gibraltar, to the Air Sea Warfare Development Unit at St Mawgan, Cornwall, and to No 236 Operational Conversion Unit (OCU) located alongside No 120 Squadron at Kinloss.

Many reasonably happy memories are held by former members of No 120 Squadron (which celebrated its 70th anniversary in 1988 and received a new Standard from the hands of the Duke of Edinburgh) of the acceptance trials of the

Above:
Flt Lt Allan Richardson in 1951.

Shackleton. Allan Richardson, a former flight lieutenant aircraft captain with previous experience on Lancaster ASR 3s, recalls that on this first flight the Shackleton seemed to have more power than a Lancaster, that it felt more solid, and that from a stability point of view was 'very smooth'. 'It felt to me to be more like flying an airliner than a bomber', he said recently.

The great delight for the pilots and others on No 120 Squadron during the acceptance trials was the amount of flying they got in. Allan Richardson recalls: 'We did about three months of something like eight hours' flying in the 24 without any "station duties" or other nonsenses. In an average week we flew on five days and had two days off. I cannot remember ever having worked so hard but we all enjoyed it.'

Left:

Undercarriage hydraulic failure on the ground was a failing among some of the early aircraft with embarrassing results such as this. The aircraft is believed to have been one from No 236 OCU at Kinloss. The problem was to some extent overcome by the fitting of jury struts, but this system could produce its embarrassments, too, as a later chapter will relate.
RAF via Roy Darbyshire collection

Bottom left:
Mk 1 'G' of No 269 Squadron *en route* for the Queen's Birthday flypast in 1952.   *Tom Silk*

Bottom:
Rehearsing for the 1952 Queen's Birthday flypast.   *Tom Silk*

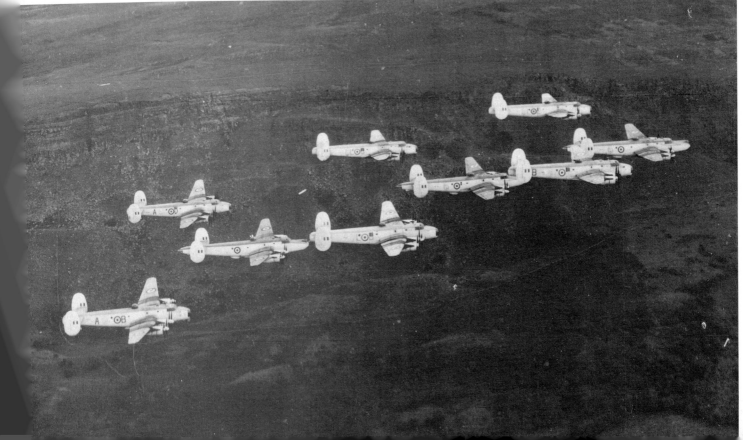

An early Mk 1 (VP256) with dorsal turrret. The inevitable soot and oil stains tended to spoil the white livery of Coastal Command at the time.   *BAe*

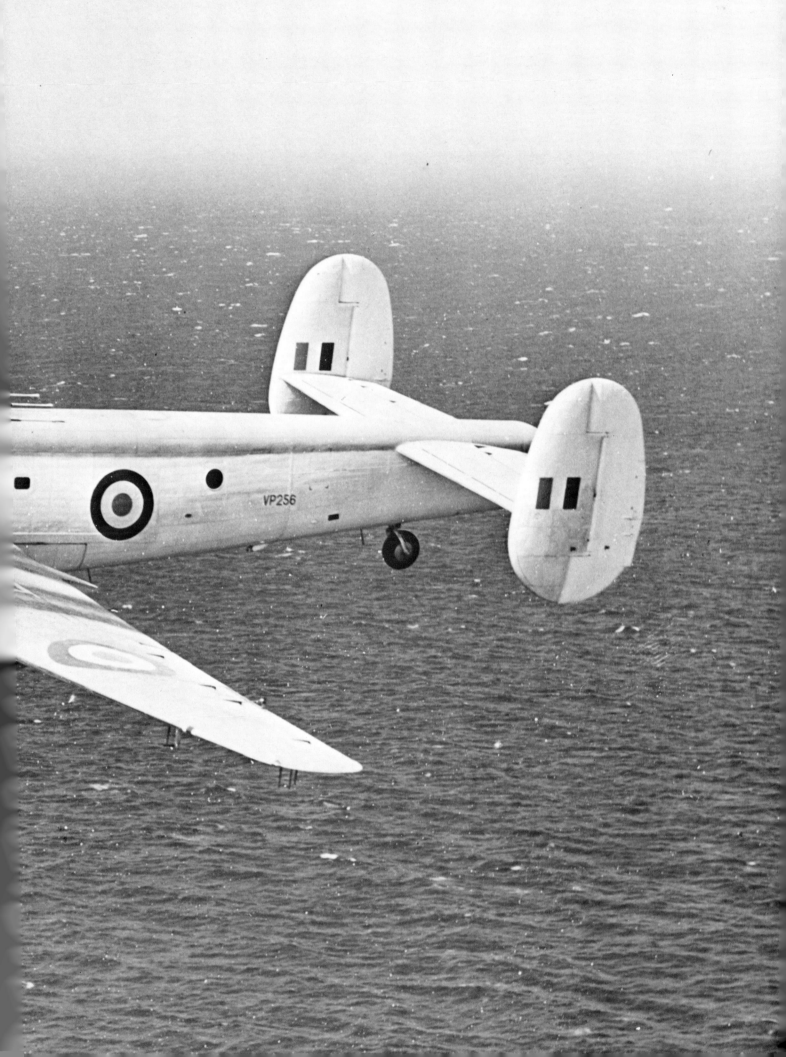

Above and above right:
Shackletons from St Eval take part in the Coronation Review of 1953. Towards the bottom of the formation photograph can be seen WL743 which was lost in a collision with WG531 during a homing exercise less than two years later. *RAF via Roy Darbyshire collection*

Right:
Shackletons at the Coronation Review of 1953. Meteors and Vampires can be seen in the foreground, whilst the background is occupied by Ansons and Washingtons.
RAF via Jim Crail collection

Wg Cdr Bryn Lewis, former Adjutant and Navigation Leader with No 120 Squadron during the acceptance/intensive trials from 1951 recalls that the whole idea was to fly the aircraft as continuously as possible. He says:

'We were to work a seven-day week for three months. The aircraft were to be flown notwithstanding minor faults so that information on engine and airframe life could be established as quickly as possible. I seem to remember that we were expected to continue a navigation sortie even if the radar had failed early in the flight. Flight lengths varied from 10 to 11 hours, down to three to four hours. My crew managed 266 hours in the three months of June, July and August of which 94½ were at night. A few crews did fly just about 300 hours.

'The aircraft was very noisy, having no insulation at all. We complained very strongly about this and a "Flying Doctor" from Farnborough came up to investigate. We started off by wrapping material around our leather headset helmets to keep out some of the noise. The Doc then had some special earpieces made for us, which helped.

'We certainly liked the extra room within the fuselage after the cramped space of the Lancaster and it was a joy to have the luxury of a galley. I recall one early sortie, scheduled for 10 or more night hours. The caterers did not know what rations they should issue to the aircrew for in-flight rations so it was decided that the Flight Sergeant "Chef" from the Airmen's Mess should attend on us. He came to the aircraft loaded with food of all sorts — potatoes, bacon, sausages, eggs, bread, tomatoes, cans of soup, fruit, beverages of various sorts, sweets, chocolates and goodness knows what else.

'The weather was not of the best and it was rather bumpy at the operational height of 800ft, but he soon set about cooking a meal for the 10 of us. In the process he did not feel very well himself but that did not deter him and he fed us like prize bulls. It never seemed to stop. There was a continuous stream of eats from the galley. I think the navigation suffered because I certainly spent too much time eating. However, this exercise was the foundation of future issues of food to Shackleton crews on long sorties.'

The first 'full prototype' Shackleton Mk 2, WB833. This aircraft was later lost in a crash in April 1968 while in RAF service (see Chapter 7). *BAe*

FLT. LT. BC. LETCHFORD

Understandably the No 120 Squadron acceptance/intensive trials did not go without incident — one 'hairy' episode is related later — but by and large the crews could find little wrong with this new aeroplane apart from noise. Inevitably there were a few returns on three engines but of course that still happens.

Looking back on his long career in Shackletons, Allan Richardson says that his 'first love' was the Mk 1. In the light of others' opinions of the various marks and phases this is intriguing. Allan himself agrees that his happy recollections may have something to do with the fact that the original Mk 1s were 'flown light' — at about 86,000lb — compared with the 108,000lb which the ultimate Mk 3 Phase 3s lifted off at. Allan remembers that his first Mk 1s virtually took themselves off with the trimmers set.

One of a number of reasons for the introduction of the Mk 2 simultaneously with the late Mk 1A production was that Mk 1s were difficult to taxy and steer accurately on the ground, with the wheelbrake controls operated by hand from points on the yoke. Toe-braking was introduced on the Mk 2s but Allan Richardson maintains that he preferred the handbrake system!

It was in fact appreciated at an early stage that some mistakes had been made in the general layout of the Mk 1s, perhaps because of the general urgency of the whole project. One of the obvious errors was the positioning of the all-important ASV (Air to Surface Vessel) 13 radar scanner in the 'chin' position. Firstly this did not provide for the desirable 360° sweep but it meant that the radome was vulnerable to bird strikes, one of which happened during a return flight from hot weather trials in Khartoum by the second prototype VW131.

Design work therefore began on the Mk 2 even before the first Mk 1s went into RAF service. The first prototype (VW126) was rebuilt at Woodford during the winter of 1950-51 as an aerodynamic prototype of the Mk 2 with a lengthened nose, a tail cone and a dummy retractable ventral 'dustbin' housing for the radar. The last device was located just aft of the main-plane rather in the style of the 'mid-lower' gun turret of the Handley Page Heyford biplane bomber of the 1930s. A little later a Mk 1A (WB833), which was eventually lost in a crash, was taken off the production line and built to Mk 2 standard and became the first full prototype.

The long nose of the Mk 2 accommodated a pair of 20mm cannon, remotely controlled from the upper lookout position and a bomb-aimer's position over the lower transparent panel. The tail cone was also made transparent to enable a crew member to assess the result of attacks by bombs or depth charges. This feature was also to become invaluable as a lookout point during search and rescue operations.

The last nine aircraft on the Mk 1A contract (the Mk 1A differed from the Mk 1 in having Griffon 57A engines all round instead of 57s outboard and 57As inboard) were completed as Mk 2s. Thereby the total of Mk 1s and 1As came

Left:
A Mk 2 of No 42 Squadron.
Alan Hall via Mike McCabe collection

Bottom left:
An early Mk 2 on a 'SHIPEX' in the Channel. The story is told of a conscientious signaller on such an exercise, briefed to challenge every vessel he saw, who flashed the code letters for 'What Ship? Whither Bound?' to a certain liner. He received the reply: 'You must be joking!' The ship concerned was RMS *Queen Mary* **on a westward heading.**
RAF via Roy Darbyshire collection

Bottom:
A No 236 OCU crew (Course 61A) at Kinloss in October 1952. Left to right: George McColl (Signaller), Plt Off Mammen (Navigator), Plt Off Holmes (Navigator), 'Shorty' James (Engineer), Roy Darbyshire (Radar/Gunner), Plt Off Fox (Pilot), Plt Off Hardaker (Pilot), Johnny Ryan (Signaller), Dave Fellowes (Radar/Gunner), and Eric Molloy (Signaller).
RAF via Roy Darbyshire collection

to 76 aircraft. A further 60 Mk 2s were built in addition to the prototype, and the nine 'line-converted' aircraft on the Mk 1A contract.

The Mk 1 serial numbers were : VP254-VP268 and VP281-VP294. The Mk 1A serials were: WB818-WB832; WB834-WB837; WB844-WB861; WG507-WG511 and WG525-WG529.

The Mk 2 serials were : WB833; WG530-WG533; WG553-WG558; WL737-WL759; WL785-WL801 and WR951-WR969.

Mk 1s and 1As were issued to Nos 32, 120, 203, 204, 205, 206, 210, 220, 224, 240 and 269 Squadrons. Others went as stated to the Air Sea Warfare Development Unit

Mk 2s of No 228 Squadron in formation while rehearsing for a 1968 Battle of Britain Day display. (This picture, like several others attributed to British Aerospace as the present copyright holders, was the work of Paul Cullerne, of A. V. Roe, one of the world's greatest air-to-air photographers.) *BAe*

(ASWDU); No 236 OCU, later styled Maritime Operational Training Unit (MOTU), and the Joint Anti-Submarine School (JASS) Flight.

Mk 2s were flown by Nos 37, 38, 42, 120, 203, 204, 205, 206, 210, 220, 224, 228, 240 and 269 Squadrons as well as by the ASWDU and the JASS Flight. Up until 1954 some squadrons flew Mk 1As and Mk 2s simultaneously.

The Mk 2s were also given 'Phase' designations mainly relating to internal fits of electronic equipment and weapons, but some exterior and visible changes were made including the eventual removal of the mid-upper gun turrets from both Mk 1 and Mk 2 aircraft.

In spite of the relative luxury of the Shackleton compared with its World War 2 predecessors, complaints continued to be made by aircrews about noise, discomfort and the level of fatigue encountered on the long sorties they were carrying out. Many of these were supported by a study carried out under the auspices of the Institute of Aviation Medicine which involved crews from No 240 Squadron.

As so often happens in the history of any Air Force, or any aviation branch of a Navy for that matter, the 'users' wanted to load more and more poundage into the aircraft in the form of weapons and other devices. The maximum weight of the Mk 2 soon went up to 95,000lb. Thoughts therefore began to turn towards a Mk 3

Shackleton (designated by the builders as Avro Type 716) and the production of Mk 2s ceased with the building of WR969.

The Mk 3 redesign was fairly fundamental, involving a tricycle/nosewheel under-carriage, wingtip fuel tanks to put the fuel capacity up to 4,248Imp gal, a 'wrapa-round' clear vision pilots' windscreen, plus a more liberal soundproofing. An internal

SECRET

The **AVRO SHACKLETON M.R.3**

LONG RANGE RECONNAISSANCE AIRCRAFT

DESIGNED AND MANUFACTURED BY

A·V·ROE & C⁰ LIMITED
E N G L A N D

HEAD OFFICE: GREENGATE · MIDDLETON · MANCHESTER   LONDON OFFICE: 18, ST JAMES'S SQUARE · LONDON · S.W.1.

SECRET

brown-and-cream décor replaced the black of the earlier marks which the Aviation Medicine boffins had identified as depressing and calculated to add to crew fatigue problems.

The 95,000lb of the final Phase version of the Mk 2 were already putting heavy demands on even the water-methanol boosted Griffon 58s during take-offs and low level manoeuvres. The Mk 3 was designed to fly at 100,000lb maximum, but the 'users' soon bumped that up to 108,000 making some form of extra assistance essential. This came in the form of Bristol Siddeley Viper jets attached to the outboard main engines. The modification posed a number of problems to the manufacturers involved, not the least being that the Vipers would have to be converted to run on high octane AVGAS rather than its 'natural' kerosene fuel, so that the necessity for two separate fuel systems in the aircraft could be avoided. It all led to some lengthy investigations at Coventry into whether the sturdy little Vipers could 'digest' AVGAS and it was decided that they could, providing that great care was taken over lead deposits on the turbine blades. This meant rules had to be laid down that the Vipers could be used for five

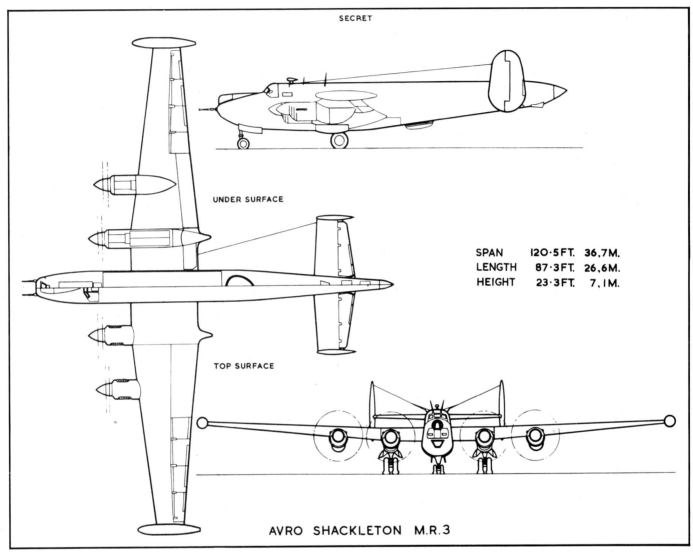

SECRET

UNDER SURFACE

TOP SURFACE

SPAN	120·5FT.	36,7M.
LENGTH	87·3FT.	26,6M.
HEIGHT	23·3FT.	7,1M.

AVRO SHACKLETON M.R.3

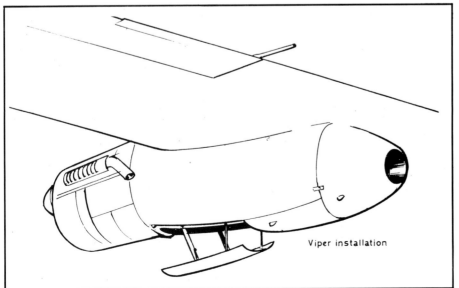

Viper installation

Top left:
A Mk 2, probably taking part in trials either at Farnborough or Boscombe Down, to judge by surrounding aircraft and absence of nose armament. *Denis J. Calvert*

Above left:
A Mk 2 of No 42 Squadron. *Peter R. March*

Far left:
The front page (marked 'Secret' at that stage) of the brochure produced by Avro for the Shackleton MR3. *BAe*

Above:
General arrangement drawings for the Shackleton MR3 issued in April 1956. *BAe*

Left:
Sketch showing the Viper installation into the later phases of the MR3s. *Rolls-Royce*

Above:
The prototype Mk 3, WR970, which crashed during stalling trials with the death of all on board (see Chapter 7). *BAe*

Above right:
Mk 3 XF708 in its natural element. *Peter R. March*

Right:
Mk 3 Series 3 XF730 with Viper jets attached. *MoD*

minutes at maximum power of 2,700lb; 20sec only at overspeed and at a total of four hours per flight at cruising revolutions. In real emergencies — and some of these occurred — the Vipers could be run at any power setting until a cockpit warning light came on.

The Mk 3 prototype, WR970, first flew on 2 September 1955 and was tragically lost just over a year later. Some early trials with it at Boscombe Down had indicated unsatisfactory stalling tendencies, especially with the weapons bay doors open. While exploring this problem and inducing stalls, Sqn Ldr Jack Wales, a senior Avro production test pilot and also the OC of No 613 (City of Manchester) Squadron Royal Auxiliary Air Force, was killed in Derbyshire together with Mr George Blake (Flight Test Engineer), Mr Charles O'Neil (Flight Test Observer), and Mr Raymond Greenhalgh (Flight Test Observer). Because of this accident the second Mk 3 (WR971) did not fly until 1956.

Three SAAF Shackletons in formation west of the Cape. The lead aircraft is being flown by Commandant James Kriel, OC of No 35 Squadron SAAF at the time. — *Louis Vosloo*

Left:
Mk 3 WR971 over the Needles. *Paul Cullerne*

Above:
Mk 3 WR972 in Royal Aircraft Establishment markings. *Peter R. March*

Below:
On 18 August 1978 a special parade was held by No 35 Squadron SAAF at D. F. Malan Airport to commemorate the 21st anniversary of the delivery of the first Shackletons to South Africa. Shackleton No 1717, one of those delivered on 18 August 1957, wore a special '21' insignia on the nose for that occasion. *Louis Vosloo*

Nevertheless the development of the Mk 3 was stimulated by the prospects of an export order with much interest in the type being shown by the South African Air Force (SAAF). In the event 34 Mk 3s of various Phases were built for the RAF under serials WR970-WR990; XF700-XF711 and XF730. Eight Mk 3 (Phase 2) aircraft were delivered to the SAAF from May 1957 onwards. (See later chapter for

their ultimate fates.) The SAAF Shackletons were, for a number of reasons, built without the Viper assistance, some of the reasons being that very long runways were available in the purchaser's country, and perhaps because some far-sighted engineers in the SAAF did not really like the idea of this form of jet-assistance, while assessing airframe fatigue and the like.

Mk 3s were flown in the RAF by Nos 42, 120, 201, 203, 206 and 220 Squadrons. (In tracing squadron allocations it is important to remember that from time to time RAF squadrons were amalgamated or disbanded. The basic policy in the 1960s was that 'senior' squadron numbers should be perpetuated, including those of the former Royal Naval Air Service squadrons always commencing with the figures of '200-plus' — thus making No 201 Squadron RAF the successor of No 1 Squadron Royal Naval Air Service.)

Some arguments may continue as to whether a total of 190 Shackletons or 191 were actually built. Absolute precision over a number of matters is difficult to achieve because of a disastrous fire at the Avro Chadderton factory in which many basic records were destroyed.

There was nearly a Mk 4 and indeed a Mk 5 Shackleton. Circa 1950 some inventive brains at D. Napier & Son Ltd, manufacturers of such historic aeroplane engines as the Napier Lion, were looking at the development of diesel (compression ignition) engines for aircraft. The Germans had after all built them and used them successfully in World War 2 and the great attraction was low fuel consumption and therefore greater range and endurance for Maritime Reconnaissance aircraft.

The inventive brains went even further into the combination of a 'diesel front end' and a 'gas-turbine back end' to be combined into the same package. The idea was to use the waste exhaust gases from the front end to light up a simple jet at the back. An engine called the Napier Nomad was built, one was fitted to the nose of a Lincoln and flown at the Farnborough Society of British Aircraft Constructors' (SBAC) display in 1951. During this demonstration the Lincoln (SX973) remained aloft with its Nomad engine alone running and its four Merlins feathered.

A Nomad 2 engine was built in 1952 and trial installations began on VW131, the second Shackleton prototype. Somewhat to the relief of the Coastal Command aircrews these experiments were cancelled because of financial restrictions; otherwise their 18 and sometimes 22hr sorties might have been extended to 36hr or more with all the aircrew fatigue problems coming up again.

In the general course of constructions and conversions a number of Shackletons were converted into trainers with 'T' designations — 17 Mk 1s and 10 Mk 2s in

Left:
There nearly was a Mk 4 and even a Mk 5 Shackleton. This picture shows Lincoln SX973 flying with a Napier Nomad engine in the nose at the Farnborough SBAC Display of 1951. It proved it could fly on the Nomad alone with its Merlins feathered. There were theories that a Shackleton powered in this way could fly forever and Coastal Command aircrews of the era were rather relieved when the project was dropped. *BAe*

Below left:
One of the Shackleton Mk 1s converted to T4s standard, WB847 is pictured serving with the MOTU — the Maritime Operational Training Unit — which succeeded the earlier No 236 Operational Conversion Unit (OCU) as a training organisation. *Peter R. March*

Below:
A Shackleton trainer, probably a T2, taking off from St Mawgan circa 1973. *RAF via Bill Burgess collection*

all down the years. Just to confuse, the converted Mk 1s were designated T4s, and the converted Mk 2s, T2s. A number of aircraft also went out of squadron service from time to time for trials and development tests at Boscombe Down, Farnborough and other research establishments so that some of the pictures in this book will show them in mysterious guises.

Above:
MOTU training aircraft from St Mawgan flying in formation over St Austell, Cornwall during 1973. *RAF via Bill Burgess collection*

Below:
Signs of the end of an era which did not end quite as soon as anyone expected. A Shackleton Mk 2 alongside Nimrod Mk 1. *Peter R. March*

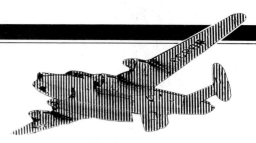

2:

Keeping the Peace

Above:
This picture marks the disbandment of No 224 Squadron in October 1966. It shows a Shackleton of the squadron overhead a Royal Navy 'Oberon' class patrol submarine on a final exercise. The relationship between Shackleton and submarine crews remained close during all the long years of 'Keeping the Peace' exercises in the Atlantic. *MoD*

In assessing the validity of this book's title one has to consider whether the Mk 1s, Mk 2s and Mk 3s of Coastal Command were really 'at peace' during their 21 years of frontline RAF service or were they 'at war', in that they were acting as a major deterrent against the growing threat of the Soviet underwater and surface fleets of the 1950s and 1960s.

Certainly the phrase 'Operational Flying Exercise' (OFE) was a well chosen one during those years, whether by accident or intention; because this was a period in world history when the Soviet Navy was demonstrating its growing power to the West. Therefore those long 18hr or more OFEs and NAVEXES imposed enormous strains on aircrews and quite a lot on groundcrews. Even more so when they began in the Shackletons from such bases as Ballykelly, Kinloss, Aldergrove and St Eval and could therefore be regarded as war operations, albeit perhaps just deterrent operations, to preserve the sort of peace of the period.

Some stories of those tasks are related in a lighthearted manner in a subsequent chapter, but it should perhaps not be forgotten that wherever Soviet-bloc submarines or surface ships moved in Northern waters during the critical years of 1951 onwards there was usually a Shackleton shadowing them. From 1972 onwards these tasks were taken on by the Nimrods — and it perhaps bears repeating at this stage that the highly efficient MR Nimrods, both Mk 1 and Mk 2, should never be confused with the ill-fated Nimrod AEW3, about which more will have to be said later.

For a description of what life was like for the crews of the Shackletons during their period of service as deterrents in what could be called a 'Shadow Battle of the Atlantic', it would be difficult to better an account written by John ('Mo') Botwood, later to become the founder of the Shackleton Association, which appeared in the February 1988 issue of the semi-restricted publication *Air Clues*. It appears verbatim with his permission and with that of the editor of *Air Clues*. John Botwood flew for most of the time with No 269 Squadron from Ballykelly and he wrote:

'Flying tasks on Shackletons in the fifties varied throughout the year, and if at the end of the year the hours flown did not balance the squadron's allocated hours, there was either nothing to do or a rush to accumulate as many hours as possible. November 1957 was typical of the latter case. No 269 Squadron at Ballykelly was short by 650hr so eight crews had to "cut them out" in three to four weeks. Each sortie became a 15hr NAVEX.

'There were three Coastal Command squadrons at Ballykelly, all equipped with Avro Shackletons. Numbers 269 and 240 were equipped with Mk 1s, and No 204 with the later Mk 2 and, although different in appearance, they had the same internal equipment. Each squadron had nine aircraft and crews and each crew comprised two pilots, two navigators, one flight engineer and five signallers.

'Our main area of operations was the North Atlantic, an intriguing part of the world with much history, both apparent and hidden. Rockall for example, the solitary landmark four hundred miles north-west of Ireland, a small rocky pinnacle sometimes 60ft above sea level and at other times completely submerged. The Royal Navy claimed it for the United Kingdom in 1952 by landing a crewman from a Sikorsky Dragonfly to plant a flag. This was one of the Atlantic's quieter days, the flagstaff was still there in 1962. Within 30 miles of this lonely rock lie four U-boat aces and many ships.

'Trans Atlantic air traffic was on the increase in 1957 and consisted mainly of Super Constellations, Stratocruisers and DC "Seven Seas". The Comet and the Boeing 707 commenced operations in September and October respectively and would soon change the scene. An average of 180 aircraft crossed the mid-Atlantic at 02.00hrs normally 20,000ft above us. We could listen to the chatter on VHF, and on HF hear the strange sounds of the four harmonic notes of the SELCAL. Many of the calls were to Ocean Weather Stations, converted corvettes which provided weather reporting to Europe and the British Isles. They could also provide direction finding, flarepaths and Ground Controlled Approaches. We would often exercise with them and practice ditchings to provide practice for their operators. Each year we looked forward to dropping the Christmas mail and tree to our "local" station, Ocean Weather Station Julie.

'A typical NAVEX would be from 06.00hrs to 21.00hrs and would start with an early morning call at 03.00hrs. Pre-flight meals in the Messes were usually bacon, eggs, sausages and beans. Then to Ops at 04.30hrs where each specialist would self-debrief before gathering in the main operations room for general briefing.

'Sorties comprised a triangular course, each leg of four hours with crew training on an opportunity basis. Cruising altitude would vary between 500 and 1,500ft depending on weather conditions.

'While the briefing was in progress, the ground-crew would have been working on the aircraft for hours. A 15hr flight required 3,626gal of AVGAS, so with no fuel jettison system and a maximum take-off weight close to 81,000lb this meant that, once airborne, we required six to

Above:
John 'Mo' Botwood, one-time signaller, mainly in No 269 Squadron, Ballykelly, later Air Traffic Controller in Australia, and 'founder' of The Shackleton Association in 1987.

Right:
A Ballykelly line scene with 'Ben Twitch' in the background. *RAF*

seven hours to burn off sufficient fuel to get down to landing weight.

'The armourers would be loading the weapons bay which had 15 stations, each capable of carrying 1,000lb except the centre station which could carry a 4,000lb airborne droppable lifeboat. A normal training load would be 32 practice bombs, six sonobuoys and four depth charges. The bombing practice was for pilots and navigators, pilots dropping from low level by eye and navigators from 300ft using the bomb sight. Sonobuoys were carried for investigation purposes and the depth charges as part of the annual allotment for proficiency training.

'You could see the results of a depth charge drop which is more than could be said for the annual drop of a homing torpedo which would enter the water with a splash, and spend the rest of the time out of view banging repeatedly against a "padded" submarine.

'The conditions under which our groundcrew worked never failed to amaze us. High winds, snow, rain and freezing cold; it was always the same. You could return with an unserviceable engine and before you started unloading the aircraft, the cowlings were off and they were working on the glowing red hot engine with frozen hands. Our groundcrew would travel with us in our aircraft when we went on detachment and 269 was always proud of the close relationship that existed between the two groups.

'It was cold in November and the passage of warm fronts provided only relative and temporary relief. The flying rations were collected by the Duty NCO and taken to the aircraft. It was quite a load as they had to provide meals for 10 men over a period that covered three main meals. The only facilities on board were one hotplate with a hot cupboard above it and a hot water urn. Most crews took pride in producing three courses for each main meal. It was amazing what could be got away with under the dim aircraft lighting. Creamed rice looked so much like scrambled eggs when served to the navigator, on toast under his yellow lighting.

'On arrival at the squadron the crew would change into flying gear. On cold sorties most would wear a pair of flannel pyjamas under their uniform, then a thick pullover, flying suit and cold weather flying jacket. A few still had the old sheepskin-lined boots which were not only warm but extremely comfortable. All safety equipment, and the crew box containing cooking utensils and cutlery would then be transferred to the aircraft and pre-flight checks would be carried out. Pilots and the engineer would carry out the external aircraft and engine checks while the navigator checked the weapons bay against the load sheet (to make sure that what they actually dropped was what they intended to drop). Signallers would stow the gear in the aircraft as their checks could only be carried out with the engines running, the power from the trolley accumulator being too weak to drive both radio and radar. If time permitted, the crew would gather some distance away to have a smoke and savour the silence. The bulk of the aircraft would loom, silhouetted against the lights of the station living quarters on the hill, making a very reassuring sight.

'The Shackleton was the last of the Roy Chadwick-designed Heavies and no one could ask for a better combination than an Avro airframe with Rolls-Royce engines. The overall dependability and surfeit of power did a lot for the peace of mind.

'When it was time to go the aircraft was entered by the door on the starboard side. Turning right to go forward you would pass the two beam lookout positions and the large stores of flares, sea markers and cameras.

'The next area was designated as the crew rest area but the two rest bunks were always full of parachute bags and more flares as this was where the illuminating flare guns were mounted. The four banks of six barrels fired 1¾ million candlepower flares at one-second intervals, lighting up any target in the surrounding area within three-quarters of a mile.

'Next was the galley and the first of the obstacles, the flap-activating housing with a cover 1ft square, then over one of the main spars past the radar station and over the big spar 3ft wide and high. Then past the navigators' and sonics position on the left side of the fuselage before passing between the engineer's position and the radio position. The two pilots' positions were next and, ducking into the nose, you arrived at the nose canopy with its bench seat for the bomb-aimer and observer.

'The engines were started in the order of starboard inner, starboard outer, port inner and port outer. With their starting, the constant roar that would stay with us for 15hr commenced. Once all generators were on-line, equipment checks could be carried out. The radar scanner was in a chin blister on the nose which allowed performance checks against the hills of Eire across Lough Foyle. Its position would also allow "reverse" GCAs. Radio contacts would be made with Group in Scotland and the sonics operators would check the performance of the SARAH (Search and Rescue Homing) equipment against a test set mounted in the control tower.

'While the navigators checked their GEE, LORAN and Decca the pilots ran up the engines and checked for mag drops. Because Ballykelly sits on an old sea floor and is surrounded by hills, everyone in a five-mile radius was more than aware of the condition of our engines. The preferred runway at Ballykelly was 26, much more favoured than 20 where the old seashore starts at the runway's end and climb-out gradient of the Shack matches the profile of the hills.

'Taxying Shackletons in fresh winds was a test of skill and strength. There was no servo assist to any control surfaces and the tailwheel was castoring, so steering was accomplished by differential braking and variation of engine power. After take-off clearance was obtained, we lined up, checked full and free movement of the controls and applied power against the brakes. Griffons at full throttle are quite impressive and when the brakes were released the long take-off run would commence.

'Once airborne most vibrations ceased and the engine noise subsided to a roar. The prototype Shackleton had soundproofing which was removed from the production models, but no soundproofing could ever help the pilots sitting in line with the eight contra-rotating propellers. The after take-off checks were followed by the engineer conducting a quick fumes check, after which all equipment would be switched on and normal routine commenced.

'Radar was manned continuously by signallers, rotating through the position. Crossing coast checks ensured that the bomb bay worked correctly. We would coast out at Inistrahull Lighthouse often, and in this case, in the dark. In the rear of the aircraft the galley would be operated on a rotating basis of every two hours. Coffee would be served as soon as possible after which silence would descend on the intercom as crew members occupied themselves with their specialist tasks. The three petrol heaters would be "fired up" (an expression that was often all too literal) and pockets of warmth established in the aircraft.

Above:
WL755 'T' A Mk 2 of No 224 Squadron. *RAF via Bill Burgess collection*

Left:
The same aircraft showing the 'dustbin' radome extended. *RAF*

'The radio operator maintained contact with Group using the Marconi TR1154/ 1155 set that was designed in the 1940s for ease of use with minimum training. Although low-powered it had a distinctive "chirp" that penetrated most static. One navigator would act as *en route* navigator while the other was ready to assume the role of tactical navigator if necessary. They would be assisted in their navigation by the radio operator with HF/DF and CONSOL fixes. Drift was measured through a vertical drift sight or the periscope mounted below the rear of the aircraft, the latter being mainly used at night with flame floats. NAVEXES became very boring for the rest of the crew and many crews practised changing positions to become proficient in other areas.

'Dawn would reveal the usual grey Atlantic with many whitecaps and large green patches where the sun shone through the clouds on to the sea. Radar would pick up Rockall at 25 miles and a radar practice homing would take place with the operator calling the overhead position with "on top, now, now, now". There was always rivalry for proficiency and accuracy, errors of even 25yd resulting in backchat among the crew. Rockall was the turning point for the southbound leg which crossed the major shipping lanes of the North-Western Approaches and normally resulted in many sightings to relieve the monotony. Radar homings were carried out on most sightings, the ASV XIII used at that time being a great improvement on the previous Mark VII. Most sightings would be freighters and small liners, larger liners like the two *Queens* and the *United States* being seen further south.

'Lunch would be prepared during these activities and low-level manoeuvring during photo runs provided interesting exercises in balancing and dexterity while eating. Our meals could consist of four courses, chicken soup followed by steak and kidney pie with potatoes, peas and carrots; finished with mandarin oranges and cream and coffee — all from tins!

'The interior of the aircraft could have been better, the matt black finish in the dim lighting becomes depressing after just a few hours — but after 15! Resting crew members found it hard to relax and soundproofing and other amenities would have improved rest and, ultimately, efficiency.

'Six hours after take-off, exercising of the propeller translation units was required. Each engine would be run through the range of boost and the propellers through the range of RPMs. This provided a welcome variation to the normal synchronised roar.

'Prior to depth charge drops, the area would be checked clear and at the promulgated time the charges would be dropped singly. Everyone would want to see the result of the drops as it really was an annual highlight. The drop would be made by the bomb aimer on a sea-marker and after release, a quick turn allowed all to see the effect of the explosion. There was a brief time interval after the weapon entered the water when a circle of white water flattened the sea with a shock wave, a tall spout reached up 60ft before falling slowly to cause a momentary halt to the progress of the Atlantic swells. All this happened in silence as far as we were concerned and, strangely, would have the appearance of slow motion. The remaining three weapons would be dropped and the sortie continued. It looked spectacular, but in reality the weapons had to be within 19ft of the target to be effective. Any attack on a submerged target had to be made within 30sec of it disappearing.

'Nine hours would have passed by this time and course would be set for home. Although the leg was four hours we would complete the detail with two hours on our local radar buoy conducting bombing practice. The intercom would again fall silent as routine was resumed.

'The heaters required constant attention and if one managed to stay on and be super-efficient it was always the one in the navigators' area, bringing complaints of it being too hot. The only crew members occupied were those involved in *en route* tasks and off-duty members passed the time as well as they could. The galley supplied coffee and sandwiches and for variation added the odd sheet of cardboard to the sandwich filling to see the reaction of those that were busy. Others off duty found their thoughts wandering as they passed the long hours. Books or other reading material were rarely carried and as many sightings were made in transit, a lookout was always maintained.

'The crew was a strange entity. New members served an apprenticeship before being accepted as capable by the rest. Although coming from all walks of life they formed a close-knit group, being insepara-

ble and looking after each other, particularly any new boy in the crew. In parts of the aircraft the cold permeated flying clothing and members moved around the aircraft to seek warm areas and find company in talking to others. This never happened on fully operational sorties when all positions were manned and everybody had a specific task.

'The sun would be setting as we headed northeast towards the coast. Radar would pick up the coastline at 45 miles confirming our tracking. The navigators would show no surprise at this (although one or two have managed to miss Ireland in the past). The course would steadily close the coastline until the loom of Tory Island Light was sighted on the horizon. We aimed to pass to the northwest of the Tory and set course for Inistrahull and Number Nine radar buoy.

'Before commencing operations, a safety check would be made of the area and communications established with Ballykelly on VHF. Radar homings started at 8-10 miles, the operator gave headings until five miles and then turns left or right until on top. Distances from three miles were called as often as possible, the one-mile call including the phrase "Flares, Flares" to start the illuminants. The bomb-aimer took over when visual contact was made and the drop made using the bombsight. Assessment of the attack was made by the observer looking rearward

through the bomb bay and was in the form of percentages under and over the target for each bomb, as they represented the start and finish of a stick of depth charges.

'A perfect straddle was with 50-50 no line error. The result was also photographed with a rear-facing camera using six photoflashes from an illuminant discharger in the beam position. Sixteen sticks of practice bombs could require a total 480 of the 1.75in projectiles to be loaded and unloaded. All this flare activity would have been notified to the Coastguard and Lighthouse services earlier in the day. From the buoy it was only 15 minutes transit to base and the lights of Derry could be seen reflected off the cloud base, but the flight had to be 15hr long so more flying was needed.

'After two hours, the transit to the circuit was made. Equipment and stores were packed, washing-up done and the aircraft generally tidied prior to landing. The crew brightened up as there was no need for debriefing and it would be straight to the Messes on return. Early morning shaves would have disappeared and all were conscious of the fact that they had been wearing heavy clothing since early in the day.

'Crossing coast checks included a visual inspection of the bomb bay with the Aldis light to confirm that there were no loose weapons or hang-ups. Circuit lengths were sometimes affected at Ballykelly by trains crossing the main runway before our arrival and the last had to be watched for. After landing a quick magneto check would be carried out before taxying to dispersal and parking under groundcrew directions. Numbers 1, 2 and 4 engines would be cut, Number 3 being used to provide services power to open bomb doors and lower flaps to rest the hydraulic system.

'When Number 3 was cut an incredible silence would descend on the aircraft although you could still "feel" the noise. The opening of the rear door brought a gust of fresh air which accentuated the "Shackleton smell"; that strange mixture of oxygen, leather, sweat, Tepol, hydraulic fluid, paint and electrics and the Elsan.

'Outside the westerly felt marvellous and everyone would soon be changed and into cars for the quick run to the Mess. Driving off one would experience the major effect of a 15hr sortie in a Shackleton — even the oldest Morris Ten would sound just as good as a Rolls-Royce.'

3:

Fighting the Small Wars

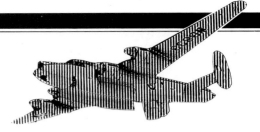

The Shackleton's part in helping to fight the 'small wars' of the 1950s and 1960s in the Middle and Far East really opened with what was termed the Central Oman Dispute which began in 1954 and went on sporadically until 1959. The Sultan of Muscat & Oman was in dispute from 1954 with one Imam Ghalib who lived and ruled inland with the Oasis of Buraimi as a key point. ('He who holds Buraimi holds Arabia' an old saying had it.) The Sultan had the support of the British and the RAF offered to back him with such aircraft as Vampires, Hunters, Lincolns, Valettas, Pembrokes and Ansons available.

In 1955 the Sultan took on Ghalib in open conflict with British support and numerous small, but sometimes vicious, actions went on for two years when the rebel Ghalib's brother, Talib, launched a force against the coast which had remained the Sultan's stronghold. By this time the RAF had added two Shackletons, part of the strength of No 37 Squadron, to its battle line of aircraft spread out between Aden, Sharjah and Bahrain.

On 24 July 1957 it is recorded, Shackletons 'entered action' by dropping warning leaflets on the Talib rebels. Venoms from Nos 8 and 249 Squadrons attacked with rockets, followed by more leaflets from the Shackletons. On 25 September 1957 it is recorded that a Shackleton

fired 50 rounds of 20mm cannon ammunition against 'dissenters'. During the period November 1957 to March 1958 Shackletons of No 37 Squadron started dropping 1,000lb bombs against such targets as water tanks, stores and aqueducts. Some of the bombing was done at night, and during the week ending 12 September 1958 it was recorded that they had dropped 148 of them.

The war went on until February 1959, the Sultan being supplied throughout with support from a wide range of RAF aircraft and by some ground troops. It was then considered that he had won and he went on to form his own Air Force and Army with considerable help and advice from the British which has of course gone on to the present day.

While the Oman dispute was going on sporadic clashes with dissident elements continued in the Western Aden Protectorate. The well established air policing techniques evolved in places like Mesopotamia in the 1930s were used to help contain them, often involving Shackletons in the leaflet-dropping and bombing roles. These clashes emanated from efforts by

dissident tribes on the Yemen/Western Aden Protectorate border to take ground and penetrate southwards, encouraged by Arab nationalist interests and to some extent by the Eastern bloc. Most of the activities took place in hostile country well north of 'Aden Colony' and up-country of such townships as Dhala and Beihan. The nature of the operations bore a strong resemblance to those on the North West Frontier, immortalised by Rudyard Kipling and others with heat, dust and rebel tribesmen sniping from concealed high ground positions and then 'melting away'.

At about this period No 37 Squadron was reinforced by its shadow, No 38, and also by aircraft from No 42 Squadron, each of these units usually having four or five Shackleton Mk 2s on strength. During the Kuwait crisis of 1961 Shackletons of No 37 Squadron were on stand-by and provided support for the substantial British ground and air forces which fended off the Iraqi claim to this oil-rich territory. There is a rather poorly documented account in existence that claims at one stage a Shackleton moved on to its bombing approach run under Air Traffic Control at

Below:
Shackletons at Sharjah. *Allan McArthur*

Bahrain civil airport, but full details of this intriguing incident have been difficult to establish.

Between 1962 and 1964 the dissident tribes in the north of the Protectorate stepped up their activities, again with the support of North Yemen, Egypt and the Soviet bloc. These culminated in some particularly fierce fighting in a pitilessly arid region known as the Radfan. Counter-measures under the codename of Operation 'Nutcracker' frequently involved Shackletons in the bombing role. During operations in the Radfan between 30 April and 30 June 1964, Shackletons flew 85 sorties, dropped 14 × 1,000lb bombs; 3,500 × 20lb; fired 18,195 rounds of 20mm ammunition and discharged 445 flares.

In spite of the weight of bombs dropped there were remarkably few confirmed reports of human casualties on the ground. The rules of 'air policing' under which warning leaflets were dropped on townships and villages were meticulously followed and the main casualties often appeared to be unfortunate camels and goats. The dried-mud buildings and walls of the up-country villages also seemed to be remarkably resistant to the blast effect of HE bombs.

The first claim of a Shackleton using a weapon 'in anger' came from No 42 Squadron in 1957 when of all things one of their aircraft was acting as an Air Observation Post for an artillery unit and for good measure strafed some dissidents with its nose cannon after receiving reciprocal directions and advice from the ground.

Towards the end of the British presence in Aden and other parts of the Middle East the main threat came from urban terrorists with two organisations, FLOSY (Front for

the Liberation of Occupied South Yemen) and the NLF (National Liberation Front) making life uncomfortable both inside such bases as Khormaksar (Aden) and particularly in the Services married quarters. At one stage there was a plan to move the Shackletons from Khormaksar, where they were large and tempting targets for terrorists, to Masira Island and Sharjah but the effective close guarding carried out by the often underestimated RAF Regiment and by Army units made this unnecessary. In fact the saddest loss of an aircraft on the ground at Khormaksar by terrorist hands was that of a very beautiful Dakota, one of the last in RAF service, which had been specially modified a few years earlier to carry the Queen on a tour of Nepal, where this type was the only one in service capable of using the short grass runways available. This aeroplane, fitted with about 10 very wide, very comfortable passenger seats and much interior mahogany trimming, had been 'acquired' by the RAF at

Aden and used to take VIPs on up-country visits, where it could land on the roughish airstrips at places like Dhala and Beihan. (The author has a very happy memory of flying in it to Dhala and back and learned with shared sadness of its demise.)

In his book *Flight from the Middle East* (HMSO) ACM Sir David Lee pays a special tribute to No 37 Squadron for the way it operated its aircraft. Sir David, who was a senior RAF staff officer at Aden himself, wrote in his book:

'The Shackleton was an extremely robust aircraft being a direct descendant from the Lancaster and the Lincoln. Its Griffon engines were well proven and the combination undoubtedly stood up to the exacting operating conditions of the Middle East with enormous credit. The aircrews did likewise as the Shackleton was heavy and tiring to fly at low level in turbulent conditions of intense heat, and these were the very conditions in which the

crews were constantly being asked to operate, for as much as eight hours at a stretch.

'Even on the Squadron's last operational sortie of 3 September (just before the disbandment) an engine was damaged by a bullet during a Search and Rescue operation and so there was no doubt that No 37 Squadron remained operational to the end.'

The climatic conditions obtaining during the 'small' Middle East wars should never be forgotten when assessing the performances of the aircraft and the men who flew them, and particularly the men who maintained them. Temperatures inside aircraft on the ground at bases like Khormaksar, Masira Island, Sharjah and Bahrain often reached 140° Fahrenheit. Blowing sand and salt-laden air contributed to rapid corrosion; totally different standards, time limits, and flying-hour limits had to be set compared with those obtaining in the United Kingdom where many of the servicing manuals had been written.

There was little relief even in off-duty hours at any of the Middle East RAF bases. Air-conditioning of living quarters

Left:
A full propeller change job — Middle East. *Allan McArthur*

Below:
No 38 Squadron groundcrew in June 1961, probably taken at Aden. *RAF*

and offices only became the norm in the early 1960s, that perhaps only because all the so-called 'peacetime' forces working in this part of the world at that time decided they had had about enough and were not inclined to take on long-term professional careers in the British Armed Forces unless living conditions got better. However, this was the period when compulsory National Service was coming to an end and the nation was looking for willing and voluntary 'professionals', so things got better in Aden and elsewhere, and they got better

Below:
Hangar work in the Middle East.   *Allan McArthur*

Bottom:
A Shackleton MR2C WL795 of No 205 Squadron on Gan Island in 1968.   *Peter R. March*

Right:
A Mk 2 of No 205 Squadron 'loaded for action' at Changi in 1968.   *Peter R. March*

Bottom right:
A Mk 1 of No 205 Squadron on improvised runway in the Far East.   *Harry Douglas*

for the air- and groundcrews of the Shackletons.

Out of all the 'small wars' in the Middle East one tribute remained to the aircrews, and especially to the groundcrews — very few aircraft were lost, NO Shackletons were lost. After the withdrawal from Aden in 1967 a detachment of four Shackletons was based at Sharjah on the Persian Gulf and No 210 Squadron operated them until the final withdrawal of the RAF from the Middle East in 1971.

Troubles were brewing simultaneously in the Far East in the late 1950s and the early 1960s and the Shackletons operated by No 205 Squadron from Singapore were in amongst the actions from an early stage. One of their main tasks was the flying of anti-piracy patrols over the South China Sea with Labuan Island off the north coast of Borneo as a forward base. Some of these 'piratical' operations were rightly suspected of being the forerunners of a larger pattern involving the smuggling of arms into the mainland of Malaya and into the British-influenced and supported states of the northern strip of Borneo. These activities were currently and later fitted into a pattern of Eastern bloc powers trying to gain ascendancy in this critical part of the Far East. The sad loss of a No 205 Squadron Shackleton with its whole crew during one of these operations will be related in more detail later.

The No 205 Squadron Shackletons played a significant part in the remarkable *ad hoc* rapid reinforcement operation which was mounted by Joint Service staffs in Singapore in December 1962. A rebel leader by the name of Azahari, supported by the Communist-aligned Indonesian Government attempted to seize the Seria oilfields in the State of Brunei. He had an immediate success by surprise and took a number of hostages, including British oil company employees and their wives. Having received much advance intelligence information, some of it culled from the reconnaissance flights carried out by the No 205 Squadron Shackletons on their

anti-piracy patrols, Far East Command at Singapore was able to mount a dramatic and successful rescue operation.

Almost anything that could fly, and most importantly any aeroplane which could carry troops, supplies and weapons was put into the air; notably the Beverley 'flying box-cars'. Some of the Beverleys landed on the grass airstrip at Seria itself, their huge rear clam doors removed and left behind at Singapore and with Scottish soldiers spraying machine gun fire hither and thither as they came to the ends of their short landing runs. The troops rapidly 'restored the situation' and all the hostages were freed unharmed.

The event however marked the beginning of what became known as the 'Borneo Confrontation' and a back-up arrangement was urgently needed. No 205 Squadron's Shackletons carried out 15 round trips between Singapore and Borneo, each amounting to about 1,200 miles, carrying troops and heavy equipment. One of the great blessings of the aircraft type's

Top:
Starting up a Shackleton MR2 of No 205 Squadron at Seletar, Singapore, just after the official disbandment of the squadron.
ANZUK PR via Bruce Robertson collection

Left:
A sign of things to come: the tail cone of a Nimrod overshadows two No 205 Squadron Shackleton MR2s at Seletar in 1971.
ANZUK PR via Bruce Robertson collection

capability to the hard-pressed logistic planners in Singapore was that it could do the round trip without refuelling. That made a lot of complicated sums much easier to solve.

The knowledge held by both air- and ground- crews of No 205 Squadron about the difficult terrain and weather conditions which they had gleaned from their earlier anti-piracy work undoubtedly contributed to the success of this often-forgotten British combined services operation.

During the remainder of the Borneo Confrontation period (1962-66) Shackletons of No 205 Squadron plus others from Nos 203 and 204 Squadrons carried out numerous long-range patrol tasks, watching activities on coastlines and spotting and recording the movements of the warships and submarines of the Communist-aligned Indonesian Navy. Many of these patrols were mounted to prevent or discourage vessels suspected of bringing troops, weapons and supplies on to the Malayan Peninsula mainland itself and they were later codenamed 'Hawkmoth'. In November 1964 No 205 Squadron logged one 'Sverdlov' class cruiser and two 'Skory' class destroyers, both of Soviet origin, while on 'Hawkmoth' patrols.

Many of these operations involved Shackletons doing the 'seeking and finding' and then directing surface ships on to targets. On one occasion a Shackleton navigator from No 205 Squadron was looking out of the window of a Hastings as he was proceeding on leave and spotted an Indonesian Navy submarine. He went to the flightdeck and under an admirable system of communication, messages were passed which enabled HMS *Lincoln* to close up with Submarine No 408 of the Indonesian Navy. The captain of the latter vessel was 'encouraged' to change course by about 180° and return to his home base.

Again the Shackleton operations in the Far East demanded much effort from both ground- and air- crews because of the climatic conditions. Average temperatures were of the order of 90° Fahrenheit, with very high humidity and many inches of rainfall almost every day and night during tropical storms.

The Shackletons' valiant troop-carrying operations at the beginning of the Borneo Confrontation were repeated in other theatres, one of the most notable being during the Suez Crisis of 1956 when five aircraft of No 206 Squadron lifted the 16th Parachute Brigade from Blackbushe to Cyprus on an 'exercise' codenamed 'Encompass'. A Shackleton could carry 33 fully armed and kitted soldiers, with heavy equipment also stowed in panniers in the weapons bay. At the end of the Suez affair Shackletons of Nos 204, 228 and other Squadrons lifted the 1st and 3rd Battalions of the Parachute Regiment, plus the

Left:
The last two Shackleton crews in the Far East prior to withdrawal in 1972. *ANZUK PR*

Headquarters of the 16th Independent Parachute Brigade Group back to the UK from Cyprus.

Those involved in the trooping operations recall that their main problem was getting into their crew positions inside the aircraft once the troops had been embarked. This usually involved stepping over, and sometimes on to, apparently inert but very live human bodies whose owners were apt to utter crisp comments in the vernacular of the Parachute Regiment.

(Trooping by Shackletons bore a close resemblance to, and the techniques were probably based on, the remarkable Operation 'Dodge' under which Lancasters took home about 100,000 time-expired 8th Army soldiers in rapid time after end of hostilities in Italy in 1945. The general system of numbers painted in circles on the fuselage floor was adopted as a 'seating plan', the actual seats consisting of the soldiers' own kitbags. The codeword 'Dodge' was adopted because of the Central Mediterranean forces' cheerful acceptance of the phrase 'D-Day Dodgers' which was probably spread by the German propaganda machine but quire erroneously attributed to a comment by Lady Astor. The 8th Army produced alternative words to the Lili Marlene song to fit the music. That is something of a digression but this author has warm memories of Operation 'Dodge', having been one of the 100,000 who got home from their war in seven hours compared with the three months that it had taken them to reach it by troopship. He has particularly warm memories of the young sergeant pilot of his Lancaster who arranged for everyone on board to get a glimpse of the white cliffs of Dover from the mid-upper turret as they neared home after four years.)

Whether or not the operation could be correctly classified as 'warlike' is open to question, but the part played by a number of Shackleton squadrons during the atom bomb tests by Britain and other Western nations between 1956 and 1958 should be recorded.

In June 1956 a detachment from No 269 Squadron took part in early experiments based on Darwin and Alice Springs, Australia; and two Shackletons of No 206 Squadron carried out eastward circumnavigations of the world while helping in the setting up of the bomb test base at Christmas Island.

Nos 206 and 240 Squadrons were involved in the 1957 Christmas Island tests and aircraft from No 224 and other units in what had become dubbed as 'the Ballykelly Wing' helped in the 1958 tests. No 204 Squadron Shackletons also played a major part in additional Australian tests on the Maralinga research grounds in 1957. Life for air- and groundcrews was again rugged and demanding, involving very long hours of work but perhaps with marginally more comfort and a slightly more kindly climate than those encountered during the Middle and Far East operations. The Christmas Island tests were codenamed Operation 'Grapple' and the Shackletons taking part carried the insignia of a red cormorant clutching a grapple hook on their fins.

The Rhodesian independence crisis of the mid-1960s produced another challenging task to some of the Shackleton squadrons involving near warlike conditions of flying and maintenance. Her Majesty's Government imposed an embargo on oil supplies reaching Rhodesia through Mozambique and the Royal Navy and the RAF were given the job of at least attempting to enforce it. Several Shackleton squadrons sent detachments on two-month tours to an airfield called Majunga in the island republic of Malagasy (formerly Madagascar) from where they flew patrols over the Mozambique Channel.

Conditions were crude and even primitive. At one stage a locally commandeered steam roller was used as a towing tractor if, as fairly frequently happened, a 40-ton aeroplane strayed off the one and only runway on to the very boggy surrounding ground.

The patrols were long and tedious and often flown in extremely turbulent conditions. The main task for the crews was to spot and identify potential embargo-breaking ships and then direct vessels of the Royal Navy on to them, all part of the basic task of MR aircraft. The operation was finally classified as successful — at least as much as any sanction enforcement one can ever be — but it did not leave many happy memories in the minds of the Shackleton crews involved.

In a summing up of the Shackleton's performance in helping to fight the small wars and in keeping the 'Big Peace' between the major powers, one might do worse than repeat the words of ACM Sir David Lee about the performance of No 37 Squadron and its aircraft in the Middle East: 'The aircraft stood up to exacting operating conditions and the crews did likewise.'

Below:
Shackleton MR1A WB828 of No 204 Squadron at Samoa in October 1958 during the atom bomb trials. *W. A. T. Burgess*

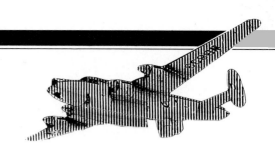

4:

Saving and Preserving Life

In the whole history of the complex art of 'Search and Rescue' (SAR) (earlier called 'Air-Sea Rescue') the Shackleton emerges as one of the most potent aeroplanes ever produced with the capability of performing this humanitarian service. In some very crude mathematics the 190 Shackletons built probably saved, helped to save, or preserved, about 100 times as many human lives as they ever 'took' in their fairly limited war operations described in the last chapter.

The total design concept of the Shackleton made it an ideal 'human eyeball' search aircraft with its downward-looking transparent positions in the nose and tail, plus numerous sideways-looking windows. It has always been capable of flying at low level in the sort of turbulent conditions that usually accompany disasters at sea — and sometimes on land — and it has always been able to carry the sort of equipment needed to aid those in distress.

The ASV (Air to Surface Vessel) radars in the Maritime Reconnaissance Shackletons were, of course, of immense value in the Search phases of SAR operations and the wide range of communications equipment often enable help to be summoned from surface ships and other aircraft. In much of the recent documentation and reporting of the SAR activities of the RAF, the Fleet Air Arm and some civilian agencies, attention has tended to concentrate on the work done by helicopters. While all the credit is fully deserved the general public has often been less aware of the enormous and essential contributions made by large fixed wing MR aircraft, in this country first the Shackleton and in more recent years its worthy successor, the Nimrod.

In the early days of single-engined rescue helicopters — Sycamores, piston-engined Whirlwinds and even the highly efficient Gnome turboshaft Whirlwinds — top cover was essential for many operations over the sea. To some extent it still is even for the twin-engined Wessex and the long range Sea Kings, particularly when they operate at extreme range. The other contributions made by the fixed wing MR aircraft fall into three broad categories, Firstly of course, there is the 'Search' phase with radar, human eyeballs and good communications all playing their part. Next, on some occasions where a disaster has occurred or is imminent outside the

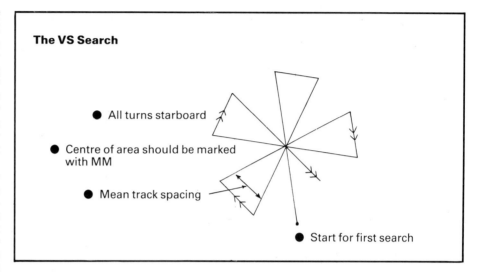

The VS Search

● All turns starboard

● Centre of area should be marked with MM

● Mean track spacing

● Start for first search

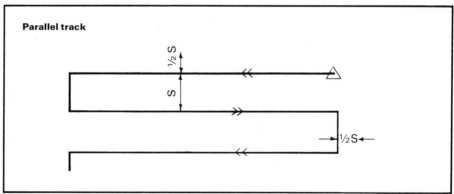

Parallel track

½ S

S

½ S

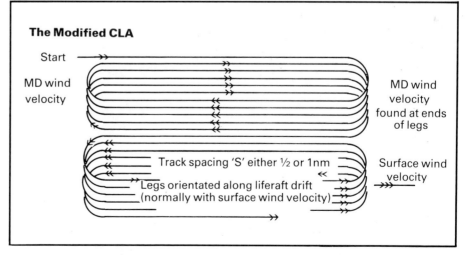

The Modified CLA

Start

MD wind velocity

MD wind velocity found at ends of legs

Track spacing 'S' either ½ or 1nm

Surface wind velocity

Legs orientated along liferaft drift (normally with surface wind velocity)

Above:

Some track patterns which have to be flown by aircraft on Search and Rescue tasks. They illustrate the stresses placed both on aircraft and aircrew particularly when flown in turbulent conditions, which they usually are.

This series of pictures illustrates the help that Shackletons could often give to ships' crews in distress. In March 1964 the North Korean fishing vessel *Chin Glongyin* caught fire in the South Indian Ocean with all her lifeboats destroyed. Shackleton WL786, which was based on detachment at Gan, took off with Flt Lt Peter Bethell as captain. The ship's crew members were seen struggling to make improvised liferafts out of oil drums and spars. The Shackleton crew made two passes overhead dropping Lindholme Gear and smoke markers. Later they homed in the British India liner SS *Nuddea* which completed the rescue.
Pictures from Flt Lt Max Dobson RAF (Retd) who was a member of WL786's crew

range of helicopters, immediate aid can be given by dropping liferafts and other aids to survival. Thirdly the MR aircraft can often be required to act as a flying co-ordination centre, guiding and controlling the movements of helicopters and surface vessels. This function, often carried out by Shackletons and now by Nimrods, means that the aircraft captain is appointed as what is usually termed 'Scene of Search Commander' or 'On Scene Commander' — often a very heavy responsibility for a young officer.

Another aspect of rescue operations not always appreciated is the strain imposed on aircrews while carrying out visual searches. By the nature of things these usually have to be done in foul weather and they have to be caried out at low level often in extreme turbulence. One of the commonly used search patterns, the 'Creeping Line Ahead', means frequent 180° turns every few minutes, imposing quite a lot of 'G' on all concerned and particularly demanding on everyone's digestive systems.

The ASR potential of the Shackleton when it was first designed and came into service was very much in the forefront of the minds of all concerned in its adoption. The prototypes were fitted for, and often carried, Airborne Lifeboats. Some of the first production Mk 1s which went into RAF service were capable of carrying these remarkable devices, and three of the Mk 3s bought by the SAAF were fitted to carry them, and indeed supplied complete with boats.

Airborne Lifeboats achieved remarkable, and hitherto almost unsung successes during World War 2, several hundred Allied airmen evading death or capture in them. Their invention has often been credited to that great yachtsman, the late Uffa Fox, but in fact he was really the perfector of an idea and a design emanating from the brain of the late Air Cdre E. F. Waring, the station commander at RAF Lindholme, Yorkshire. Almost simultaneously he had invented an air-droppable liferaft system named 'Lindholme Gear', still in use to the present day, to which many hundreds owe their lives.

The fitting of Airborne Lifeboats (the Saunders-Roe Mk 3 version) to the prototype Shackletons and some of the early production Mk 1s was a logical development because their immediate predecessors, the Lancaster ASR3s, had carried them and ASR was very much a prime role for Coastal Command in the late 1950s. The lifeboats were not retained because it was assessed that in peacetime their main asset, that of enabling downed crews to get away from enemy coasts and out of minefields, was not going to be relevant.

Air-droppable liferafts, particularly those assembled in the Lindholme Gear configuration were clearly going to be more effective and simpler to use. Lindholme Gear in fact consists of one fairly large liferaft to which are attached a number of other floating 'packages' all joined together by lengths of floating rope. One of its most important features is that, when dropped correctly, the gear will

either drift down on to survivors in the water or they will drift into it, the floating rope wrapping itself around those concerned. They can then pull in on it, board the central dinghy, and then recover the survival 'goodies' packed into the other containers, It was a brilliant concept by Gp Capt Waring back in the 'forties and the equipment in current use, consisting of a nine-man central dinghy and three survival packs, differs very little from that used in the later stages of World War 2.

Above:
The Saro Mk3 Airborne Lifeboat as fitted to three of the South African Shackletons on display at the SAAF Museum, Pretoria. *Louis Vosloo*

Below:
An inflated Mk 9 dinghy of the type which forms the 'core' of the Lindholme Gear.
Bruce Robertson collection

Right:
Lindholme Gear packs plus some of the survival 'goodies'. In 1988 there was correspondence in *The Times* protesting at the proud name of RAF Lindholme being sullied because the name was retained when it was converted into a prison and it obtained much publicity because of a disturbance there. Certainly within the RAF it will always be remembered both as a bomber station with a proud wartime record and as the 'home' of this device which has saved hundreds of lives and continues to do so. *RAF Kinloss*

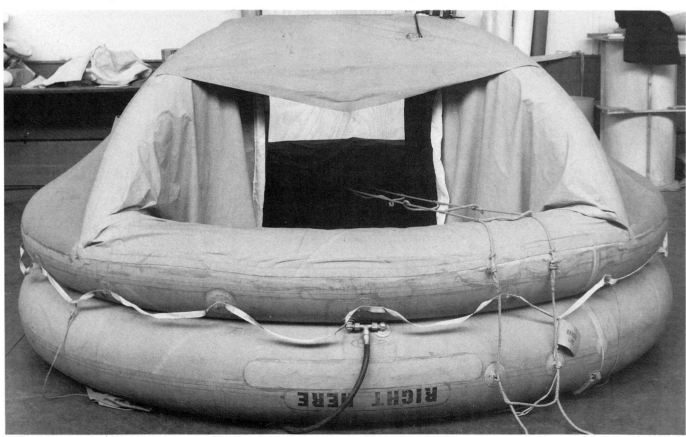

One of the main advantages of Lindholme Gear over the Airborne Lifeboat in peacetime conditions was that it could be loaded, without much difficulty, into almost any large or medium-sized aircraft which possessed a weapons bay or some large doors.

A good deal of skill and airmanship is still needed to drop Lindholme Gear effectively. The aircraft captain has to assess wind and wave conditions, the state of survivors in the water — whether, for example, they are already in some sort of liferaft or lifeboat or perhaps just floating in lifejackets or clinging on to flotsam — and then decide whether the gear will 'drift

down' on those in the water or whether they will 'drift up' into the Gear. (Similar calculations, of course, had to be made when dropping Airborne Lifeboats though with rather different factors involved, the latter having a remarkable system of self-acting rockets which would place sea anchors in the correct position, inflate watertight compartments and even throw out floating ropes for survivors to grab.)

The MR Shackletons normally carried one set of Lindholme Gear at all times; those on specific SAR tasks or on standby would have at least two loaded. This general practice is followed to the present day in the Nimrods. To this day, too, the

last of the AEW2 Shackletons of No 8 Squadron carry a set of Lindholme at all times. Although not committed to SAR tasks there obviously could come a time when one of these aircraft was in the right place to assist in a maritime disaster, perhaps while flying a barrier patrol over the North Sea or the Faroes Gap, both potential areas for such events.

One of the earliest 'life-preserving' tasks allocated to the Shackleton MR squadrons during the middle 1950s and early 1960s was that of escorting the piston-prop transatlantic airliners of the period — Constellations, Stratocruisers and the like which were apt to suffer at least single-engine failures or problems. There were many occasions when Shackletons from Ballykelly, Aldergrove or Kinloss were despatched to the middle of the Atlantic to give escort and general comfort to an airliner with a problem. Often these jobs could be frustrating for the Shackleton aircrews in that, having punched their way against a westerly airstream for several rough hours, they would make a rendezvous with an airliner flying on three engines and on turning round eastwards the latter would streak ahead for the safety and comfort of Shannon, or thereabouts, while they were hard-pressed to keep up with it on all four Griffons going well. Nevertheless all those operations were taken in good part.

A very serious and very unpleasant event of this sort took place in September 1962 when a Super Constellation with 57 American servicemen, seven of their wives, two children and eight crew aboard lost three of its four engines off the southwest coast of Ireland and ditched. Fifty of the souls on board reached liferafts, many of them injured and suffering from skin burns from the petrol-polluted sea water in which they had been immersed for some time. Soon after the SAR operation had been mounted the survivors were spotted by a Shackleton doing a visual search which then directed a freighter ship, the *Celerina*, to them. By the time this ship reached the scene six survivors had died in the liferafts and 17 were in urgent need of hospital treatment.

RAF and United States rescue helicopters were guided on to the *Celerina* by Shackletons and winched the worst injured casualties off the ship's deck and got them to hospital quickly in the Irish Republic. Some were given interim treatment in the sick bay of a British aircraft carrier which happened to be in the vicinity. It was a 'best possible' rescue operation, certainly assisted in the early stages by the ability of Shackletons to seek and find their targets.

The rescue of a number of survivors from a disastrous fire on board the Greek-owned cruise ship *Lakonia* in December 1963 was in a large part due to the work done by the crew of Shackleton Mk 2 WL757 of No 224 Squadron, which scrambled from Gibraltar at first light after the ship's SOS had been received. The crew, whose captain, David Leppard (now Air Cdre), found the ship burning from

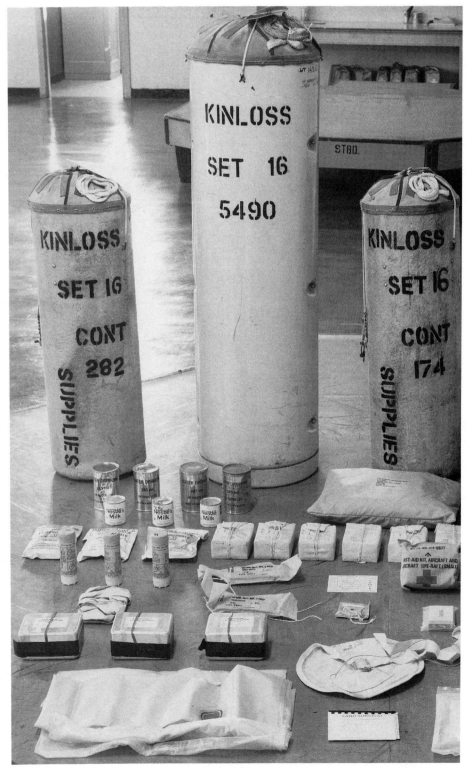

stem to stern and could see numerous lifeboats in the water, some clearly containing survivors, others apparently only holding dead bodies. They dropped both sets of the Lindholme Gear and saw some survivors climbing aboard one of the main (central) dinghies. They were then able to carry out the tasks of co-ordinating the movements of other rescue aircraft and surface ships. In the event 128 people aboard the *Lakonia* died but more than 900 survived, many of them perhaps because of the efforts of David Leppard and the crew of Shackleton WL757.

An unusual, and sadly unsuccessful, rescue attempt inland was made by a Shackleton of No 37 Squadron in July 1962 when a Beaver aircraft of the Desert Locust Survey Organisation was reported overdue up-country in the Western Aden Protectorate. The crashed aircraft was spotted by Flg Off Burden and his crew and they dropped an item called a CLE (Container Land Equipment) by para-

chute. This piece of equipment carried by all Shackletons and many other aircraft types during the Middle East conflicts consisted of about 400lb of survival items including fresh water.

Flg Off Burden and his crew saw a ground rescue team approaching the aircraft wreck in Land Rovers and guided

it in by dropping messages in weighted bags. They also saw what appeared to be the dead body of the Beaver pilot near the aircraft wreck. It transpired that the pilot had survived the crash but had been killed by local bandits for what they could loot from his pockets. It was a sad ending to a good effort by all concerned and the incident was probably one of the few in which a CLE pack was dropped by a Shackleton on a SAR mission.

Perhaps one of the most important life-preservation missions involving Shackletons occurred just after the earthquake at Agadir, Morocco, in 1960, in which 12,000 people were killed. The Shackleton Mk 2s of No 224 Squadron based at Gibraltar were among the aircraft of many nations which flew in with such relief supplies as food, medical equipment and tents; and then flew out with survivors, usually to French airfields. There were some occasions when newly-born babies were tenderly washed in the aircraft galleys and their feeding bottles sterilised in the tea-making machines. One of the sadder tasks for a No 224 Squadron Shackleton was the flying in of 2,400lb of quicklime for use in the necessary communal graves.

One very significant contribution made by Shackletons to the whole art of SAR was the development of various homing

Left:
The *Lakonia* on fire. *R. D. P. Milwright, who was the navigator of WL757*

Above:
A 'SARBE' (Search and Rescue Beacon) evolved via 'WALTER' and other devices.
Burndept Radio

Below:
The world's last three flying Shackleton MR3s lined up at their base at D. F. Malan Airport. The South African bid to obtain spares in spite of the arms embargo because these aircraft were frequently used for SAR was unsuccessful. *Louis Vosloo*

devices, at first carried almost exclusively by downed airmen but later made available to yachtsmen and others in trouble on the High Seas.

Shackletons took part in early experiments with a device called 'Walter', which did not work very well, partly because its signals could be confused with emissions put out by broken submarine telephone cables. Next came the much more effective SARAH (Search and Rescue Homing) beacon, which led on to the very efficient SARBE (Search and Rescue Beacon) and then on to even more efficient devices, of about the size of a cigar packet carried by most combat airmen.

The steady development of rescue — now sometimes called personal locator — beacons down the years owes much to those early trials by Shackletons. The present almost worldwide system means that an airman or a mariner in possession of one will probably be found within a few hours, even in the middle of the Atlantic Ocean.

Rescues, masterminded by MR Nimrods at Kinloss saved the lives of several sailors taking part in a single-handed transatlantic yacht race in the summer of 1988, largely because of the locator beacon system which now feeds into orbiting satellites. If anyone had survived the disastrous mid-air explosion which occurred in an Air India Boeing 747 on 23 June 1985 well off the West coast of Ireland, they might have been rescued. The Kinloss standby Nimrod was overhead bodies in the water a little over an hour after the aircraft had been reported as missing from radar screens.

One of the more curious proofs of the efficacy of the system occurred a few years ago when a reporting station in France picked up a beacon signal via satellite and identifying it as coming from South-West Scotland. Under the well-oiled system the Rescue Co-ordination Centre at Pitreavie, near Edinburgh, launched a Sea King helicopter. The Sea King picked up beacon emissions which led it to the middle of a housing estate in central Glasgow. The signals were loud and clear and obviously emanating from one particular house to which police officers were directed.

A personal locator beacon, which was part of a trawler's safety equipment, was found bleeping away merrily in a wardrobe and the occupant of the house had a little explaining to do as to how he had come into possession of it. Nobody in the SAR world minded very much: even if it had been an expensive 'exercise' it at least proved the system. (For some time the Armed Forces resisted the sale of personal locator beacons to yachtsmen and other mariners because of the risk of false alarms, but in the event the extension of the system to civilians has resulted in the saving of many lives and very little false alarm wastage.)

The SAR aspect loomed large in the decision by the SAAF to purchase the eight Shackleton Mk 3s in 1957. The South African Government had responsibility for safety over some of the busiest sea lanes in

The Shackletons . . . and after ?

This cartoon appeared in **The Cape Argus** of 22 November 1984 when the problem of obtaining spares for the SAAF Shackletons under the arms embargo reached its height. The case was unsuccessfully made that the SAAF Shackletons were predominantly SAR aircraft. The accompanying caption to this picture read:

'No one can be happy, except possibly the Russians, at the news that after 27 years of meritorious service patrolling the Cape sea route the Shackletons, this country's only specialised maritime reconnaissance aircraft, have made their last operational flight.

'During these years the Shackletons became a living legend, famed for their reliability and honoured for the many lives they saved in search and rescue operations under the most difficult conditions.

'Starved of spares by a UN arms embargo, only the great dedication and ingenuity of their groundcrews have kept these old planes operational for so long. But now they have had their day, and the world's nations — and especially crews who round the Cape of Storms — could well be the losers.' *The Cape Argus/L. Vosloo*

(Author's note: This cartoon and the accompanying text are included for objective judgement only. Neither this, nor any other of my books, have any political motive behind them, hidden or otherwise.)

A nose-radar equipped DC-3 of No 35 Squadron SAAF is seen alongside a grounded Shackleton in 1985. These aircraft have become known as 'Shackotas' or 'Dackletons'. *Louis Vosloo*

the world, those around the Cape of Good Hope. They are also among the most perilous.

The South African Shackletons were involved in a number of spectacular rescue missions during their period of service. In 1965 one of eight Buccaneer Mk 50s on a delivery flight from the UK to South Africa lost both its engines at high altitude over the South Atlantic and both crew members had to eject into a waste of water. Two SAAF Shackletons took part in the rescue mission and the two crew members of the Buccaneers were picked up by a surface ship after Lindholme Gear had been dropped to them by one of the Shackletons.

In August 1975 a SAAF Shackleton was briefed to the effect that Portuguese refugees from the civil war in Angola were making their way south in small boats. Capt Van Dyke and his crew took off in

This view of the first full Mk 2 prototype of the Shackleton — WB833 — illustrates the aircraft type's potential in the 'Search' role. Note the downward viewpoint in the nose, the transparent tail cone and at least one side-view window visible. The radar housing is fully extended downwards giving the aircraft an immense search potential, and the weapons bay doors are open; through them lifesaving devices such as Lindholme Gear could be dropped.
BAe via Bill Burgess collection

Right, top to bottom:

Dropping mail to the Ocean Weather Ships was a regular task for Shackleton crews in the 1950s and, while perhaps not coming strictly under the heading of 'preserving life', it certainly preserved morale for the ships' crews. This series of photographs shows the briefing taking place for the Christmas Eve drop on *Weather Watcher* in 1954 — Flg Off Birnie, Flt Lt Bryn Lewis and Flt Lt Paddy Green at rear; the drop itself; and some additional cheer going out in the form of carols over the radio. On the left is the late Sqn Ldr Ross the Kinloss Padre, and Cadet Wallace, now an airline captain.

The Weather Ship mail runs were classified as valuable navigational exercises and much care was taken to achieve precision in the final drop, if possible placing mail sacks within boathook reach.

Wg Cdr Lewis collection

Shackleton No 1720 and found some 200 refugees around the mouth of the River Cunene, and about 40 small vessels at sea which had been overloaded and were obviously in peril. They also saw the word 'BREAD' marked out on the same near the river mouth. They and other aircraft dropped food containers and kept track of the refugee vessels for the next 24hr.

When the South African Shackletons were nearing the end of their operational hours in the middle 1980s, and the arms embargo prohibited the supply of spare or technical back-up from the UK, one of the cases put up from Pretoria was that these aircraft were primarily required for the humanitarian task of SAR around the Cape, and that they were not 'weapons of war'.

The case failed, however, on the grounds that Shackletons can indeed be weapons of war as bombers or submarine hunter-killers, and one by one the seven SAAF aircraft (one was lost in a disastrous crash to be recorded in detail later) had to be grounded. Of all things the SAAF then had to convert DC-3s (Dakotas) to take on the SAR task around the Cape.

The last recorded SAR operation involving a Shackleton occurred during the Scottish blizzards of 1977. A chartered Jet Ranger helicopter carrying a film cameraman was forced down on a frozen loch at dusk and the uninjured pilot and passenger set off to walk towards help in a temperature of −5° Centigrade and in fading light. A rescue operation was mounted from the Pitreavie Co-ordination Centre and at about 9pm the crew of an AEW Shackleton of No 8 Squadron at Lossiemouth spotted the tiny lights of 'miniflares' which the helicopter pilot had fired from the mouth of a cave shelter he and his companion had found. As a result of this sighting — a great tribute to the efficiency of the 'eyes' on board the Shackleton — an RAF Whirlwind rescue helicopter reached the two men during the night. The rescue helicopter itself nearly ran into trouble because of steadily deteriorating weather but all were eventually safely 'gathered in'.

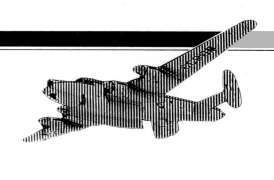

5:

'A Funny Thing Happened . . .'

One of the joys of writing this book and its predecessor, *Avro Shackleton*, has been the response to appeals for anecdotes about the aircraft. They have come not only from all parts of the United Kingdom but from Australia, New Zealand, the United States and South Africa. One of Nature's gifts, especially vouchsafed to former warriors and servicemen, seems to be to remember firstly and most vividly the funny aspects of adversity or hardship. This tendency has displayed itself, one feels, in the case of many of the 'Shackleton Tales'.

The formation of the Shackleton Association in 1987 and the publication of its newsletter (now entitled *The Growler*) has enhanced the exchange of such stories. The very first newsletter contained this contribution from No 8 Squadron RAF, about which much more later in this volume:

'You are old Father Shackleton,
The Young Nimrod said.
But the hardy old Shack
Just shook his wise head.

'You'll have to get some in lad,
Oe'r land and oe'r sea
And get barnacles on your belly
When you're flying low like me.

'I'll tell you something else lad,
And this is not a tale.
The Shackleton is the only plane
Whose crew can harpoon a whale.

'A Russki sub to the Kremlin
Sent an urgent SOS:
"If these Shackletons come lower
They'll be drinking in our Mess."

'Seaweed on the wing tips,
The radome salty and white,
Props churning up the wave tops,
A real pilot's delight.

'No smelly, stinking paraffin,
And yowling, yelling jets,
We may not have fancy trimmings,
But on us you can place your bets.

'Your father was a Comet,
That I can't deny,
But my Dad was a Lancaster
Who helped to free the sky.

'So next time you come in lad,
And enter up your log,
Remember that compared with me,
You're just a blinking sprog.'

During Operation 'Grapple' a Shackleton took-off with a jury strut (the device designed to prevent an unwanted retraction of the undercarriage legs on the ground) still in position. Another Shackleton was scrambled as a 'chase' aircraft to warn the crew of the first one and carry out a visual inspection before a landing was attempted. In the general haste both jury struts were left in position in the chase aircraft. All must have eventually ended well but it has been recorded that on the night in question the following words were sung alongside the Christmas Island strip by Shackleton people. They went to the tune of 'Island in the Sun'.

Shack taxy out from the little hut,
In one wheel was a jury strut.
Shack take-off into the morning sky,
One wheel hanging, way on high.

Chorus:
Oh Shackleton over the sea,
Given to me by the Air Ministry.
All my days I will sit and gaze
At your undercarriage that will not raise.

Next Shack take-off into the blue,
With undercarriage locked down too.
Crew all think it's a fuse gone phut,
But everyone know it's a jury strut!

Chorus:
I see Shack going round and round,
Skipper wishing he was on the ground.
When making sure that the door is shut,
Always look for the jury strut!

Chorus again!

The following story which is best regarded as 'apocryphal' and regarded with some suspicion by this author, but nevertheless worth the telling, concerns Shackleton 'G' for 'George' with a Polish captain aboard joining the circuit at St Eval. There were some overcrowding problems on the Eval runway and Air Traffic Control asked 'G': 'What is your endurance? Over.' Alleged reply from Shackleton 'G': 'My insurance

is Prudential. Why you want to know? Over.' ATC Controller (sotto voce): 'Oh God, he's at it again.' Followed by: 'G-George, hold your position. Over.' Reply from G-George: 'Ock Kay, Ock Kay. Going into reverse. Over.' Air Traffic Controller to Squadron OC (in the Tower by this time): 'Well at least we know his insurance company.'

The Shackleton Association newsletter began a 'Records' column in its second issue. It noted the 'highest' as being 27,200ft in WL738 on 7 June 1955 by John Elkins. It went on to state that the 'fastest' was 200yd in five seconds by Dinty More, Pat Miller, Jack Perigo and Mo Botwood on the occasion when the depth charges fell out of the bomb bay on to the dispersal concrete at Ballykelly on an unrevealed date.

Sqn Ldr Mike Duiguid, the SENGO (Senior Engineering Officer) of No 8 Squadron at the time of writing recalls that visitors from other NATO Air Forces in the 1980s sometimes had difficulty in adjusting to the internal comfort arrangements of an AEW Shackleton, compared with those provided in 'shirt-sleeve-environment' aeroplanes to which they were used. An Elsan was an object which they had not seen before. 'On one trip one of our guests managed to use a flare chute, another preferred an oxygen tube,' he recalls. 'We could only conclude that they must all have been pretty tall chaps, or perhaps knew how to stand on their toes like ballet dancers.'

During the Borneo Confrontation period, six attempts were made one day in 1964 to get WL748 serviceable and airborne from Labuan Island. After all had failed the aircrew adjourned to the transit tent. The detachment Technical Officer strode in shortly after them, soaked in sweat, and grabbing a mug of the essential hot sweet tea, declared: 'That bloody aeroplane should be melted down and made into saucepans.' Voice from the back of the aircrew group: 'And then they'd leak'.

Sqn Ldr (Retd) Tom Silk remembers that while serving as a Radio Operator/Air Gunner in 1952 on the OCU (Operational Conversion Unit) at Kinloss he and the rest of his all-NCO aircrew took off on an

Above:
A Shackleton-eye view of 'Ben Twitch' near Ballykelly. *Bill Burgess collection*

Below:
Signal at green for the train? The famous 'Ballykelly Railway'.
M. Henderson via David Hill collection

Operational Flying Exercise with the dubious privilege of dropping four depth charges that someone had found in a possibly unstable condition in a corner of the station bomb dump. 'They looked decidedly moth-eaten and of old age,' he recalls. 'We were duly briefed to drop them singly at something like 150ft at 160kt near a radar buoy in the Moray Firth. A Royal Air Force pinnace would act as Range Warden, clearing the area of fishing boats — for some reason the fishing was always good around the radar buoy.'

The crew arrived and saw the pinnace having typical trouble with the local fishing folk who did not want to abandon a fairly lucrative livelihood just for the sake of the RAF and its tricks in the Moray. A low pass by the Shackleton with bomb doors open did not seem to impress the fishermen much. However a clear area was found, the pinnace informed of the crew's intentions, a smoke float released and the first depth

I was going to cook "SOLE VÉRONIQUE : FILLETS OF BEEF À LA POMPADOUR and CHILEAN LECHE NEVADA but I lost the BÉRCHAMEL SAUCE so you'll have to make do with bacon and eggs - again

Above:
The things that can happen when you put a galley into an aeroplane.

charge dropped at the recommended height and speed.

'I was in the mid-upper turret and was more than a little startled to see a column of water climb up behind us to at, or perhaps slightly above, our own height,' Tom Silk told me. The aircraft captain, Sgt Eric Dawson, decided that the depth charge had exploded on impact with the water and that the recommended dropping height the crew had been given was probably dangerous.

'We circled while a decision was taken on what would be a safer height,' Tom Silk remembers. 'We were amused to see the fishing boats heading off — as one — to their home ports at speed. The remaining charges were dropped from a higher altitude but they all exploded on impact,

too. However, the RAF pinnace seemed to do some rather good fishing itself shortly afterwards.'

Many Shackleton funny reminiscences (perhaps 'funny-peculiar' rather than 'funny-ha-ha') emanate from that notable base, RAF Ballykelly, referred to elsewhere in this book; the home of a number of Shackleton squadrons loosely called 'The Ballykelly Wing', and one of the first operational bases for the type.

Ballykelly, located on the south shore of the Foyle estuary in Northern Ireland, had been selected in 1941 as one of the jumping-off bases for Coastal Command during the Battle of the Atlantic. One of the features of Ballykelly was (and remained until it became an Army base

under the proud name of Shackleton Barracks circa 1972) a flat-topped mountain named on maps as Benevenagh, upon which a number of wartime aircraft came to grief in bad visibility. The Shackleton crews quickly renamed it 'Ben Twitch' and always gave it a generous offing during take-offs and approaches.

The other special characteristic of Ballykelly was the main Belfast-Londonderry railway line, which on a World War 2 expansion of the airfield, crossed the 'preferred' Runway 26. Aircraft and train movements were controlled remarkably efficiently by a joint signalbox/airfield control tower arrangement which worked well for many years. In railway terms the block section extended 7½ miles from Limavady Junction to Eglington.

During World War 2 a scheme was evolved, with the assent of the Ministry of Home Affairs, for the construction of a signalbox at the runway/railway crossing, providing 'distant, outer and home' railway signals, all linked with Flying Control in the Ballykelly Tower. The *modus operandi* was that when Flying Control wanted the runway for an aircraft they would ask for it by a prescribed bell code. If the railway signalman did not expect a train to pass within five minutes he would 'release the runway'. There were various interlocking safety precautions which present-day Air Traffic Controllers might envy — the railway signalman for example could not leave his 'commutator' to 'Ring Clear' for the runway unless all his running signals for trains were set at 'Danger'. When Flying Control had finished with the runway, a Shackleton or something similar having landed and taxied away, the Controller would then turn his commutator to 'Runway Closed' and thus advise the railway signalman.

There are no records of any even near-misses between Shackletons and railway trains at Ballykelly but many crews remember being invited to make a few circuits at the end of 18hr 'NAVEXES' and the like because a train was due and this did not exactly please them. Some old Shackleton hands tell tales of having to look out for tyre-destructive debris at the end of the runway in the form of broken bottles when there had been a contest on the football fields of either Belfast or Londonderry.

Ballykelly is also the source of many tales of the somewhat fractured relationship between the RAF and the Royal Navy during the immediate postwar years. It lay hard by an establishment called JASS (Joint Anti Submarine School) at HMS *Sea Eagle*, the shore base just outside Londonderry, which became Ebrington Barracks at a very early stage of the latest round of troubles in Northern Ireland.

A great many Coastal Command Shackleton aircrews — many of them all-NCO crews, some of these comprising a fairly high proportion of ex-Bomber Command prisoners-of-war, cheerfully dubbed 'Kriegies' by their friends and not noted for

their acceptance of precise discipline — lived under the Rules and Regulations of Her Majesty's Navy in peacetime. It was not always a happy arrangement according to those who experienced it; but as usual the general sense of humour of British Service personnel rose to the occasion. Some of the Shackleton crews having worked out of Ballykelly on 18hr flying exercises were not amused by being expected to leap out of their beds on the appearance of a young naval officer on his 'rounds' in the middle of the morning.

Apparently they seldom actually did so and eventually both sides accepted the arrangement.

A tale is told of a Shackleton sergeant signaller about to leave HMS *Sea Eagle* for some well-earned relaxation in Londonderry being told by a Master-at-Arms that the Liberty Boat was not due to leave for another 30min. He then declared that he was rowing himself ashore and would come back the same way, perhaps well after 23.59hrs. Nothing more was ever said, except by the former sergeant signaller

who has regaled the author with many such tales. This was all part of the fun which characterised the early Shackleton operations in Coastal Command.

In July 1956 Sgt John Cordy of No 220 Squadron was part of the crew of Shackleton WB825 ordered to search for yachts which were overdue during a Channel race and scattered in a storm. They found a yacht, named *Uomie*, lying to a sea anchor with sails down and no signs of life on board. They homed a nearby merchant ship on to the yacht by Aldis lamp signal and returned to base. Two years later John Cordy was summoned to his station commander's office at RAF Upwood, where he was then working as a Link Trainer Instructor, and handed a solemn letter from the Air Ministry under Reference A. 304968/58/F.78/CHB saying he was entitled to £7 0s 4d as his gross share of a salvage award relating to the yacht *Uomie*. The station commander handed out the money in cash but drew his attention to the final paragraph of the Air Ministry letter which stated that Income Tax would be dealt with at a later date by HM Inspector of Taxes (Public Departments 4) Cardiff, to whom details of the award were being notified.

John Cordy, now living in New Zealand, says that the tax deduction was made on his following week's RAF pay parade. He was glad to tell me this, because I had warned him that he might be due for extradition to the UK for non-payment of taxes having disclosed his story to me in a letter.

A substantial proportion of the humour concerning operations in Shackletons appears to have emanated from that remarkable feature of Type 696 — the galley. Apart from some rudimentary arrangements in Sunderlands and perhaps occasionally in Catalinas, the Shackleton was really the first aeroplane ever supplied to the Royal Air Force with a galley. There was never any formal establishment for a

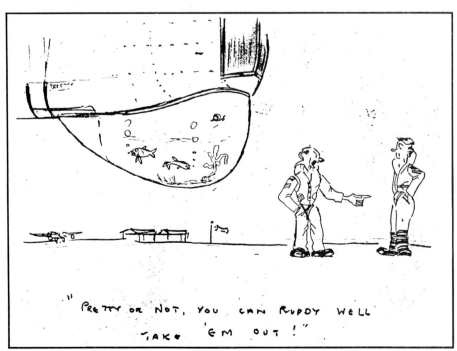

cook to be employed aboard but very quickly various crew members, most of them signallers, decided to take on this extra-mural activity.

The opportunity provided to plan for, cook, serve and above all consume hot food and drink in flight, put all the early Shackleton crews on their mettle. Quite apart from the enjoyment of such consumption, and its very important part in maintaining human efficiency on 18hr plus sorties, it became a wonderful way of relieving boredom, both for those preparing and cooking the food and for those consuming it. 'Galley stories' abound in Shackleton folklore. Some are illustrated graphically in this chapter. There are tales of dishcloths catching fire above galley stoves; of soup spilt down aircraft captains' flying boots.

Plastic fried eggs of the kind obtainable from joke shops figured in many stories, including one in which such an object was served — by what is called 'Sod's Law' — to a Secretary of State for Air while flying as a passenger. The insertion of strips of cardboard into sandwiches has already been referred to by John Botwood.

Whether or not it could be called a 'funny thing' remains open to doubt, but certainly a 'funny-peculiar' thing happened to the crew of an Aden-based Shackleton carrying out one of those air-policing tasks when it did its *coup de grâce* strafing run with its nose 20mm guns over an emptied village. A stray camel ran across the gunner's line of fire and much to his astonishment it exploded in a tongue of flame. The air gunner was upset because he was something of an animal lover.

On return to Khormaksar all was explained by the skilled intelligence officers who were acquainted with what went on up-country. Apparently one of the stratagems (nowadays repeated by many other smugglers of various sorts) was to mix suitably wrapped packets of explosives into camel feed, take the animals innocently through check points, and then recover the contraband after the due process of nature. The rather upset Shackleton nose-gunner was informed that he must have just hit a camel with a bellyful of gelignite or something similar.

Flt Lt S. M. Partridge, now of RAF Odiham, recalls an occasion when an important Shackleton sortie had to be abandoned because a kettle would not stop boiling. It occurred while the Shackleton was waiting to take-off for a rehearsal of the Queen's Jubilee Royal Review flypast in 1977. A Victor jet bomber parked alongside then radioed to say that there was a plume of steam issuing from a vent in the starboard side of the Shackleton fuselage. An urgent investigation by the Shackleton crew revealed that in spite of it being switched off, the galley boiler was still steaming away. All attempts to isolate this piece of equipment from the main electrical system failed — indeed the crew had to keep topping-up the boiler with cold water to prevent a burn-out and possible fire risk. Eventually all systems had to be

shut down and the back-up Shackleton called forward for the rehearsal. Flt Lt Partridge recalls that there were then some inevitable comments from the Victor crew about steam-age aeroplanes.

One of the most noted raconteurs of funny Shackleton stories is Mr Alister More AFC, AHHA, still alive and very well and living in Farnborough. Mr More (naturally known as 'Dinty' in the RAF) spent one of the most colourful parts of a long RAF career as a sergeant signaller in Shackletons. Later he moved on to become a winchman in rescue helicopters and won his AFC helping to rescue seamen off a sinking ship. 'Dinty' More's memories are prolific and photographic. Some of his tales were recorded in *Avro Shackleton* but at

least three deserve repetition and perhaps an even longer posterity record in this volume.

One concerns the occasion when he and his crew were engaged in an exercise searching for 'enemy' submarines provided by the Royal Navy. They spotted a surfaced submarine off the coast of Norway and carried out a 'simulated' bombing attack on it. 'Dinty' More recalls that at the time they were short of the little 5lb practice bombs that were supposed to be used on such occasions, but had some rather noisier 25pdrs aboard, which they did not think the Royal Navy would mind too much, so they dropped some around the submarine's conning tower.

At the debriefing they reported what they had done but the Royal Navy representatives queried their report on the

Below:
. . . and another.

"H-HOW DID YOU KNOW I-I W-W-WAS A S-SHACKLETON P-PILOT?"

Above:
Master AEOp Alister 'Dinty' More, *raconteur extraordinaire* **of Shackleton tales, with his family at Buckingham Palace after receiving the Air Force Cross for his part in a helicopter rescue at a later stage in his career.** Hull Daily Mail

grounds that they had not put an exercise submarine in that position. Photographs were produced and studied. The debriefing became hushed while it was assessed that a Soviet submarine had been 'exercise-attacked'. There were some worries about this all becoming a major international incident, but it was finally discovered that the Soviet submarine was itself exercising in Norwegian waters. In the event nobody had been hurt — except perhaps the eardrums of some Soviet Navy officers in the conning tower of their ship when the 25pdrs exploded around them, and nothing more was said.

'Dinty' More also remembers the occasion when he and an all-NCO crew of a Shackleton were ordered to take-off from an airfield under American control. They were not best pleased to be doing this job, having only recently completed a long OFE (Operational Flying Exercise) and had had little sleep. They were even more displeased when they received no reply from Flying Control on asking for clearance for take-off.

Silence reigned aboard for a few minutes until the flight sergeant captain of the aircraft declared over the intercom words to the effect of: 'Oh never mind. Engineer — give me full power for take-off of all four, kick me up the posterior and off we'll go again.' Those words are, for publication purposes a polite interpretation of what he

80

actually said. The unfortunate part was that there was an internal fault in the aircraft radio system under which the intercom conversation was being 'broadcast' at full power and a number of very senior officers monitoring the exercise heard it all. In one of 'Dinty' More's favourite phrases, certain senior officers were 'not amused'.

There was the other occasion when 'Dinty', as the sergeant signaller, was checking out messages just before take-off on a routine exercise from St Eval. Into his headset came a 'NATO Mandatory Diversion' signal. This was not something which could be ignored in the 1950s. It was in five-letter cypher form and 'Dinty' thought he had got it right until he did some decoding and realised that just one letter could have made all the difference between them being ordered to fly to Jacksonville, Florida, or to Ballykelly, Northern Ireland.

Under the rules applying, 'Dinty' More had no opportunities to make any checks.

There were some discussions between him, his navigator and the aircraft captain and they all settled to go to Jacksonville, Florida, rather than Ballykelly, Northern Ireland. 'Dinty' More recalls some shortening of his fingernails, especially after they landed at the Azores to refuel and nobody there seemed to know anything about them, even if they were refuelled. He remembers contemplating an alternative career in the Sanitary Branch of the RAF as they approached Jacksonville after a few more refuelling stops. He then remembers the glorious welcome from the USAF at Jacksonville, which included a complete personal re-kitting for the whole crew in lightweight, hot-weather clothing, and knowing that he HAD got the message right after all.

(*Author's note to this chapter:* As stated at the outset some of the stories told above might not stand up to critical examination, but they are all worth the telling, after the passage of some time.)

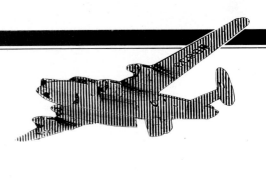

6:

'A Hairy Thing
Happened to Me . . .'

Although its record speaks for itself in terms of reliability and ruggedness, the Shackleton did of course give its crews some 'hairy moments'. As the next chapter sadly has to relate, the aircraft type also figured in a number of tragedies. This section of the book should not be taken as any reflection upon the design of, nor the workmanship put into, the 190 Shackletons that were built. That such events occurred was largely the result of the demands put upon the aeroplane and upon the crews who flew the type.

The Shackleton was after all a hastily developed version of a high altitude bomber, produced in a hurry to meet an urgent demand, and then through much of its service used to carry out low level operations in its R and SAR roles. No wonder then, that there were a number of hairy moments, and a rather high rate of Category 3 accidents — those beyond repair by squadron recources.

Curiously one early failing on the Mk 1 Shackleton had nothing to do with its performance in the air, but because it was extremely difficult to taxy on the ground, especially over the sort of muddy terrain which could be encountered off the runways at the early postwar Coastal Command stations. Former Flt Lt Allan Richardson, one of the No 120 Squadron pilots involved in the acceptance trials, has one or two 'hairies' in his ample stock of memories.

At an early stage of the trials he was flying a Mk 1 'J' on a navigation exercise off Cape Wrath when a generator came loose in No 2 engine nacelle, shorting out a busbar in a spectacular manner which he likened to a private, internal thunderstorm. He was well out at sea and a TWA airliner relayed his May Day signal and then closed up to escort him at 1,000ft to Reykjavik civil airport in Iceland. He achieved a straight-in emergency landing by the headlights of two lorries and stopped about 100yd from a cliff edge.

In November 1956 in a Mk 2 Allan Richardson encountered engine trouble because of extreme cold during a sortie off Norway, checking on the movements of Russian submarines believed to be heading for the Mediterranean.

He then encountered severe icing and a lightning strike which put all his radio compasses and most of his communications out. He climbed above cloud but could not descend back through it because he had

almost run out of de-icing fluid. Again he was helped by a civil airliner, this time of Iceland Airways, through which his dedicated radio operator, Master Signaller George Burns, was able to relay messages to Norwegian bases and obtain replies. Eventually by dint of three-way relayed radio conversations they were guided into Olande through 50kt winds and an 800ft cloudbase, where they stayed for three days until engine changes and other repairs were carried out.

The retractable 'dustbin' radar housing on the Shackleton Mk 2s and Mk 3s accounted for at least two 'Phew - w' type incidents.

Flt Lt (Retd) Ken Brooke of No 38 Squadron was flying as second pilot in Mk 2 WL740 'Y' from Malta on 4 September 1959, on a Mandatory Training Sortie involving radar homings on to merchant ships plus other tasks, with Flg Off Gil Harman as captain, a crew of 10 and three Royal Navy passengers. When the time came to retract the radome from the fully down 'attack' position it would not move. despite valiant efforts by Master Engineer 'Taff' Stockwell, which went to the lengths of seamanlike rigging together of ropes attached to hydraulic jacks and radio conversations with expert engineers on the ground up to the officer commanding the Luqa Engineering Wing, the radome remained firmly down.

Knowing that the ground clearance of the fully extended radome could only be a matter of inches at best, even if the main undercarriage legs remained almost at full travel, and aware that the fuselage was by then full of a fine, highly explosive mist of evaporating hydraulic fluid, there was some tension aboard as the emegency landing was contemplated. They orbited Malta for four nail-biting hours to burn off fuel, removed and stowed all side escape hatches, sat the passengers and themselves in firmly strapped crash positions and alerted the airfield emergency services.

They made a six-mile straight approach on to Runway O6 and Gil Harman made what Ken Brooke describes as a 'pussy-pissing-on-silk' wheeler touchdown. There was not so much as a squeak from the still extended radome on the tarmac but Ken Brooke does recall that they shut down the engines and got all the electrics switched off in record time and were later rather glad of a crate of beer produced by an understanding Sister in the Medical Centre

whence they had all been taken for a check on the 'wobblies'.

Perhaps the best documented, but still repeatable, radome incident was that involving Flt Lt Bill Houldsworth (later well known as one of the captains of the Battle of Britain Memorial Flight Lancaster *City of Lincoln*) and his co-pilot, Bill Howard who is still flying charter aircraft in Scotland. Returning from a long Atlantic training sortie in April 1961 in WR957 of No 204 Squadron they were asked to round off their day and night by carrying out an exercise attack in darkness on a buoy moored off the Donegal coast. It was a very dark and stormy night and at the end of their standard radar and sodium flare approach to the recommended 300ft attack altitude the bomb-aimer called that he had lost sight of the target in the spray and the back-glare from the flares.

Bill Houldsworth (later Squadron Leader, now retired, and one of the 10,000hr-plus 'aristocrats' of the Shackleton world) remembers that he lifted his head momentarily from his instruments to give some final guidance to the bomb-aimer then lowered it just in time to see his altimeter going below 50ft. The events which followed consisted of the two 'Bills' feeling a heavy impact upon which they both pulled back on their yokes, followed by a call from the radar operator that he had lost his picture. This was rapidly followed by another call from him to the effect that the loss of picture was not surprising because he had also lost his radar scanner and most of the radome. The next cry came from a crew member in the tail cone complaining that his flying boots were full of sea water.

However, WR957 climbed away and they returned to Ballykelly where they circuited until daylight so that ground observers could see that enough was left intact of their aircraft for a safe landing which was duly made. Bill Houldsworth remembers that somebody did 'slap the back of his wrist' over this episode, but his distinguished career was certainly not in any way jeopardised. This demonstration of the strength of the Shackleton did much to maintain the confidence of other crews in the aircraft type.

Jim Crail (mentioned elsewhere because of his long association with Mk 2 WL747 still flying with No 8 Squadron) remembers a night exercise in a Mk 1 when soon after take-off petrol fumes seeped into the

cockpit. They were identified as emanating from an inspection panel just under Jim's First Pilot's seat. All unnecessary electrical equipment was switched off but the fumes were so overpowering that Jim had to open a small clear-view panel on the windscreen in order to breathe.

The aircraft was at an all-up weight of 86,000lb and therefore about 10,000lb above maximum landing weight. Jim Crail decided, however, that he would have to land quickly, never mind the weight, and pulled off what he describes as the smoothest landing in his entire flying career. After they had all breathed in fresh air and relief it was found that a cross-fuel cock, or possibly a drain cock, in the bomb bay had jammed open. They had lost 300gal during the circuit and they had depth charges aboard. An hour later they were airborne again on a major NATO exercise.

That very well informed publication *Roundel* recently recorded an event in February 1957 when HRH Prince Philip was a 'participant observer' of NATO exercises in the Mediterranean for which task he flew from Gibraltar in a Shackleton Mk 2 (WR968 'D' of No 120 Squadron). The Prince, having flown during the morning of 28 February, was deposited at Gibraltar and the aircraft used for a routine squadron operation later the same day.

At the intended end of this flight the crew discovered that the starboard undercarriage leg would not lock down. As a result Gibraltar instructed the crew not to land there for fear of damaging installations and other aircraft on the ground. The aircraft was diverted to Port Lyautey, French Morocco (now known as Kenitra)

where it spent four hours burning off fuel before lining up for a foam carpet landing on the right-hand side of the runway. However, the setting sun rendered this attempt too hazardous and, while further fuel was burned off, the other side of the runway was foamed. WR698 landed well on the port gear but as the starboard wing came down the aircraft swung off the runway and ploughed to a halt in a storm ditch. Another 'Phew -- w -- w' one! What if His Royal Highness had been aboard?

The hairy moments which Shackleton ground-crews sometimes endured (especially when flying in them to some remote location) have been well described by Jim Hughes of Elgin, who served for 30 years in the RAF as an engine fitter, 12 of them working on Shackletons. He was involved in the Operation 'Grapple' nuclear bomb test episode in 1958 while a sergeant engine fitter on No 240 Squadron, Ballykelly.

'Despite some wintry weather the first two aircraft left on 1 February. Everything went well until an engine failure caused one plane to return to Travis in California where an engine change was diagnosed. A spare engine was required and the spare aircraft, WG509, of which I was I/C ground crew, was authorised to transport it to California.

'At that time Shackleton Mk 1s could carry a spare engine in the bomb bay but it necessitated removing the old bomb doors and replacing them with a special set which had a slot cut in them for the engine to stick out. Changing the bomb doors was not a particularly technical job but it involved a lot of manpower and as the signal had arrived on a Saturday it was some time before a motley crew had been assembled to do the job.

'Those of us who were travelling were allowed home for some sleep before reporting to the aircraft in the early hours of Sunday morning. We were just in time to see the engine being hauled into position and the awful realisation that the doors had been fitted back to front. Murphy's Law had triumphed and while the NCO I/C prepared to commit Hari Kiri another gang started to repair the damage.

'Monday morning saw us scramble aboard with fingers crossed, but the initial ground runs found low boost on No 1 engine. At first our fitters could find nothing wrong but one bright lad found a broken pipe in the bomb bay — the result no doubt of some ham-fisted rigger fitting the bomb doors. This was soon rectified and just before noon we roared off over Benevenagh ("Ben Twitch" to all Ballykelly hands) into the wintry darkness bound for Larges in the Azores. To say the aircraft was crowded would be an understatement.

'As well as the normal crew we carried extra aircrew, a full groundcrew of eight men plus three fitters to do the engine change at Travis. These latter also had their engine change kit in a large coffin-like box which would not fit in the bomb bay and had to be jammed inside against the main spar.'

Jim Hughes' saga goes on to report many other vicissitudes during what added up to an 11-day journey including 69hr 10min flying time with calls at Bermuda; Charleston, South Carolina; Barksdale, Louisiana; Sacramento, California; and Hickham Base, Honolulu. When they finally got to Christmas Island they discovered that a Hastings from No 202 Squadron at Aldergrove had got there before them with another spare engine. Nevertheless, they and the rest of No 240 Squadron 'kept 'em flying' until the conclusion of the bomb tests.

Two other especially 'hairy' incidents were recorded in *Avro Shackleton*. They not only deserve, but really need, repetition. They are the sagas of Lisbon Bridge and Culloden Moor.

The Lisbon Bridge saga occurred on 13 December 1967 when Flt Lt Michael Bondesio of No 203 Squadron was bringing Mk 3 WR987 home to Ballykelly after some exercises in the Mediterranean.

They had flown through a sandstorm between Malta and Gibraltar and when they were about 90 miles northwest of Lisbon the translation unit (the critical part of the contra-rotating propeller arrangement on a Shackleton's Griffons) failed on No 1 engine.

Left:
All that was left of Bill Houldsworth's radome after hitting the sea. *RAF*

Below:
The nosewheel arrangement on the Mk 3s sometimes caused problems — especially if the gear did not lock down. This happened to the SAAF's 1722 at Langebaanweg Air Force Base in July 1960. *Louis Vosloo*

Above:
No 1721 had to make a belly landing at Ysterplaat in September 1962. The aircraft was repaired. *Louis Vosloo*

Right:
'Fell at Culloden'.

Michael Bondesio (who was later to die tragically from a heart attack while flying in a SAAF Shackleton) jettisoned fuel from the wingtip tanks and sent a PAN call to Lisbon civil airport.

No 1 engine was feathered but the propellers continued to rotate slowly, presumably because of the translation gear failure and added to drag. The Vipers were prepared for start-up but the flight engineer then reported that No 4 engine had developed a severe oil leak and would have to be shut down too.

Fuel jettisoning was stopped and only the port side Viper 'lit'. If the starboard jet had been started, even with the cessation of fuel jettisoning, there would have been a serious fire risk from the oil pouring out of No 4.

Michael Bondesio was therefore left with power from two Griffons and one Viper giving 100% power on its 'emergency only' setting with occasional 'rests' down to 40% being imposed by the flight engineer.

Permission was given for a direct approach on to Runway 03 at Lisbon and

the crew map-read their way over strange ground through a smoke haze. The crew at the front of the aircraft then saw to their astonishment the recently erected Salazar Bridge in front and a bit above them, this structure not being marked on their charts.

Michael Bondesio turned away from the bridge to try to gain some height but without much success — entirely understandable with the limited power resources at his command. He was then contacted by the Portuguese captain of a TAP Boeing 727 who led him on an alternative route across the outskirts of the city to the airfield. Shackleton WR987 finally put down at 120kt, a final problem being turbulent jetwash from the 727 which had had to overshoot after its 'Good Shepherd' act.

That emotive word 'Phew-w-w' was actually used in the report of the incident published in Coastal Command's flight safety magazine. Michael Bondesio was awarded the Air Force Cross for coolness and airmanship.

Operating all over the world inevitably involved Shackletons with some of the worst forms of weather that can be encountered over the earth's surface. During the Beira patrol days Air Cdre David Leppard recalls his Mk 2 becoming caught in a 'revolving tropical storm' with a 70 millibar drop on the barometer and winds gusting to 140kt. They survived but he is apt to say that the encounter may have taken about as much off their life expectancy as it put on to the airframe fatigue life.

Above:
Mk 3 XF730 of No 206 Squadron approaches the Gibraltar runway towards the bottom left of the picture. The Times

Of all the 'hairies' the experience of Flt Lt John ('Pop') Gladstone and the crew of Mk 3 XF710 of No 120 Squadron on the night of 10 January 1964 remains in the forefront of aviation history and deserves re-telling.

They took off from Kinloss for a routine night exercise and almost immediately encountered overspeeding of No 3 engine, which eventually caught fire, broke from its mountings and fell into the sea.

A few seconds later a fire warning light showed from No 4 and it had to be feathered.

In the 'worst possible' situation of two engines out on the same side (one very literally 'out') 'Pop' Gladstone and his second pilot Flg Off J. A. W. Lee skidded the aircraft clear of Inverness which had been directly in front of them. By the light of the flames from one burning wing they managed to see a relatively smooth patch of Culloden Moor and put the aircraft down, all souls on board managing to get clear without serious injury.

One of the signallers, Sgt Jamie Hamilton, conscientiously grabbed his log and took it out with him, later to complete the 'Termination of Flight' section with the words: 'Fell at Culloden'. (Sgt Hamilton was killed a few years later in a Vulcan accident.)

The event is still remembered in the village of Smithton on Culloden Moor whose inhabitants succoured the crew of

'710' with some traditional Scottish hospitality, it so having happened that a bit of a barn dance was going on at the time. Flt Lt (later Sqn Ldr) Gladstone was awarded a second Bar to his AFC.

In spite of it having been one of the type's first overseas 'homes', Gibraltar has never been a favourite spot for Shackleton crews with its shortish runway tucked alongside the rockiest part of 'The Rock' and some complicated low level manoeuvres required to make an approach without violating Spanish air space. (For that matter it is not all that popular with any aircrew.)

On 14 September 1957 No 224 Squadron's Mk 2, WL972, was due to perform a low flypast during a Battle of Britain anniversary display on The Rock.

In those days Shackletons were permitted to display their capabilities by carrying out flypasts with one, or even two, engine feathered.

On this day, four miles out and at 500ft No 3 engine oversped in WL972. (At one period engine overspeeding was a fairly recurrent problem on the type.) Partly because of the general noise going on aboard there was a failure of communi-

cation between the first and second pilots and No 4 engine was feathered instead of No 3. A snap decision at the front end resulted in a spectacular wheels-up arrival which was loudly applauded by the crowd, many of whom thought they were watching an engine-feathered display with special effects. (Later the undamaged back end of '972' was 'stitched on' to the front end of WL796 which had been damaged at Aden, thus causing some confusion to collectors of registration numbers if nothing else.)

The first complete write-off of a Shackleton was in fact recorded at Gibraltar in August 1951 when VP283 of No 224 Squadron hit the ground short of the runway and shed its main landing wheels. The belly landing was finally consummated on a nearby beach without injury to the crew or anyone else.

'Jimmy' Orrell (the Avro Chief Test Pilot at the time) remembered being despatched to Gibraltar to give some advice on the low level handling of the aircraft during the necessary complicated approach patterns. The crews of No 8 Squadron still regularly call at Gibraltar with their AEW Mk 2s but they treat its 6,000ft runway with much respect.

7:

The Tragedies

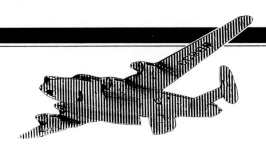

Shackletons were involved in 14 catastrophic and fatal accidents with 141 lives lost. Four of these accidents occurred in the six months between November 1967 and April 1968 and the Under Secretary for Defence (RAF) at the time, Mr Merlyn Rees, had to answer a private member's question in the House of Commons on the type's safety record. He was able to state that there was no evidence of a single common factor and certainly none of fatigue in the airframes which had respectively flown 5,971; 3,620; 3,814 and 2,525hr. These were all low figures compared with the total life envisaged in the design and all the aircraft had undergone major refits.

As with the Category 3 accidents mentioned previously and with some of the 'hairies', if there was a common factor at all it was the operationally inevitable one of a heavy aircraft, first conceived in shape as a high altitude bomber, being used on tasks which called for low level, sometimes quite violent, manoeuvres over sea and land. One fatal accident, already referred to in Chapter 1, resulted in four deaths and occurred during the always hazardous business of test flying, particularly when 'unnatural' conditions such as stalling have to be induced. Another, involving the loss of two aircraft and 18 lives, was probably the result of a mid-air collision, again

under the special conditions encountered by MR aircraft. Two were probably due to extreme weather conditions. One was attributed to engine overspeeding (as stated in the previous chapter a fairly prevalent fault during one stage of the aircraft's history). Two other deaths occurred during Shackleton operations, those of an engineering officer who fell from an aircraft while it was taxiing and was run over; and of a crew member who fell through an escape hatch.

The loss of Mk 2s WG531 and WL743, both of No 42 Squadron on 11 January 1955 was of course the most catastrophic of all the fatal accidents and in some ways the

Shackleton Accidents

Date	Mark and Serial	Squadron	Place and circumstances	Suspected cause
25/06/52	Mk 1 VP261	No 120 Squadron plus No 240 Squadron crew members	Atlantic, on ASW exercise. 12 killed	Possible loss of power during low-level manoeuvres
8/10/52	Mk 1 VP286	No 236 OCU	Moray Firth. Air/sea gunnery exercise. 14 killed	Stall in steep turn during low-level attack manoeuvres
11/12/53	Mk 2 WL746	No 240 Squadron	Off Argyllshire coast on exercise. 10 killed	None declared
12/02/54	Mk 2 WL794	No 38 Squadron	Mediterranean on NAVEX from Malta. 10 killed	None declared
11/01/55	Mk 2s WG531 and WL743	No 42 Squadron	Irish Sea during exercise from St Eval. 18 killed	Mid-air collision during homing exercise
7/12/56	Mk 3 prototype WR970	Hawker Siddeley	Derbyshire during stall trials. Four killed	Loss of control during essential stall trials
10/01/58	T-4 VP259	MOTU	Hit trees during roller landing practices. Two killed, four hurt	None declared
9/12/58	Mk 1 VP254	No 205 Squadron	South China Sea during anti-piracy patrol from Labuan Island. 11 killed	Loss of 'orientation' during low-flying over glass-smooth sea
8/08/63	Mk 3 1718	No 35 Sqn SAAF	Hit mountains in turbulence and icing during exercise. 13 killed	Icing, turbulence, encountered during 'short cut' over mountainous terrain to resume part in international exercise
8/12/65	Mk 3 XF704	No 201 Squadron	Crashed into Moray Firth 8nm (15km) north of Kinloss during GCA let-down. Eight killed	None positive
4/11/67	Mk 2 WL786	No 205 Squadron	*En route* Gan-Changi. No 4 engine failure followed by wing fire. Eight killed, three rescued	Overspeeding of No 4 engine
19/11/67	Mk 3 WR976	No 201 Squadron	Hit sea during anti-submarine exercise from St Mawgan during descending turn. Nine killed, one rescued	None positive. Possible pilot error
21/12/67	Mk 3 XF702	No 206 Squadron	Hit ground Creag Bhan, Lochailort, Inverness-shire. 11 killed	Extreme turbulence and icing
19/04/68	Mk 2 WB833		Hit ground Mull of Kintyre during joint exercise with submarine. 11 killed	Navigational error

most puzzling. The two aircraft left St Eval, Cornwall, at 10.14 and 10.20hrs respectively for a patrol and search exercise to the south of the Fastnet Rock which should have lasted 15hr.

The first aircraft, captained by Flg Off George Board was 14min late taking off and the second (captained by Plt Off Wood) left early, thus reducing the normal half-hour separation time to 6min. However, there was never any evidence to suggest that this could have contributed to whatever happened many hours later. Indeed radio messages were received indicating that the two captains had adjusted their separation and that up to 20.00hrs on the night of 11 January they were flying at the prescribed 85 miles distance from one another.

Ground contact was lost from 20.58hrs when a radio operator failed to receive a reply from Plt Off Wood to a message containing barometric pressures over the exercise area. Neither aircraft made its scheduled 21.00 or 22.00hrs situation reports. Almost anything that could fly from all the air bases in the southwest of England took off at the first light on 12 January to search and all surface ships in the sea area were advised of the overdue aircraft.

No trace was ever found of wreckage or bodies until more than 11 years later when the starboard outer engine of WL743 was caught in the net of a trawler off the southwest coast of Ireland, about 75 miles from the point which the Board of Inquiry estimated as a probable impact position if there had been a mid-air collision. Although much of the inquiry work had to be based on speculation, one theory was that the two captains had decided to carry out radar homing exercises on each other and that this had led to a collision. The inquiry finally judged a mid-air collision as 'the least improbable' cause but the matter still troubles the No 42 Squadron OC of the time, Sqn Ldr Norman Wilson, now living in retirement in Southport. He has never been entirely convinced by the mid-air collision theory and in 1988 he was preparing to lead a small pilgrimage to the village church in St Eval where there is a memorial to the 18 lost members of the squadron in which he took so much pride.

Some particularly touching events followed the loss of Mk 1 VP254 of No 205 Squadron in the South China Sea on 9 December 1958. This aircraft, coded 'B', took off from Labuan Island, Borneo, at 05.48hrs on an anti-piracy patrol of the

type described in the 'Small Wars' chapter. The captain was Flt Lt W. S. Boutell with a crew of nine aboard plus Mr A. R. Miller, the Acting Deputy Police Commissioner of North Borneo.

Soon after take-off the aircraft was ordered to investigate a report that some shipwrecked fishermen were stranded on an atoll about 280 miles north of Labuan. At 07.10hrs Flt Lt Boutell radioed that he had located the fishermen and had diverted a junk to their assistance.

At 11.45hrs he reported that rescue operations were going ahead and that he was going to revert to his original task in 15min. He sent a position report at 11.59hrs and nothing further was heard from VP254.

An extensive air and sea search was mounted and on the sixth day of it Flt Lt John Elias, also of No 205 Squadron (eventually the 'top scorer' on the type with 13,000hr) saw the letter 'B' and the figures '205' marked out in white coral on the sandy beach of Sin Cowe Island at 09.53N/114.20E. A frigate of the Royal New Zealand Navy, HMNZS *Rotoii*, was in the area and taking part in the search and she put a landing party ashore which found a single grave marked with a simple wooden cross on which 'B 205' had been carved. An RAF cap and an aircrew watch were pegged down by stones nearby.

A little later a helicopter from the carrier HMS *Albion*, also in the area, arrived and exhumed one body from the grave. They

took it and the simple little cross back to their ship. It later transpired that the crew of the Chinese fishing vessel *Ray Fu Chen* had seen the Shackleton crash into the sea shortly after it had circled them. They had noted its fuselage markings of 'B' (its letter code) and '205' (its squadron number). They had hastened to the point of impact and recovered one body, which was that of FS D. N. G. Dancy, the flight engineer, plus the cap and the watch, but nothing else.

Assessing that there would be an air search, the skipper of the fishing vessel, Capt Gan Chung-Huang, took the body and the other relics to the nearest island where he arranged a Christian burial, organised the making, carving and erection of the cross and then with special perspicacity made his crew lay out the aircraft markings in white coral on the beach.

FS Dancy's body was first taken to the RAF cemetery at Singapore and re-buried in a plot there on 19 December 1958 in the presence of the C-in-C Far East Air Force, AM and Earl of Brandon. The cross was re-erected beside St George's Chapel at RAF Changi where it stood until 19 August 1971 when, on the final British withdrawal from the Far East, it was flown back to the UK in the last Shackleton of No 205 Squadron to leave.

The cross was finally placed in the little church at St Eval, which has of course become something of a shrine to many Shackleton people as well as to their Sunderland predecessors and others of Coastal Command. A plaque in the church records the names of all the crew of VP254 and a framed document outlining the above story.

Capt Gan Chung-Huang was eventually traced by Her Majesty's Consul at Tamsu, Tainan, and rewarded with a letter of thanks and some gold for himself and his crew. His name is regarded highly within the RAF, especially amongst old 'Shackleton hands' of the Far East Air Force.

The cause of this crash remains in some doubt. The most likely explanation is that Flt Lt Boutell had encountered the problem experienced by many flying boat captains back to World War 2 — that of flying over a mirror-calm sea with no immediate visual reference as to his height. An alternative which had to be considered is that the official 'passenger' on board, the police officer, might have stumbled over a fuel cock at a critical moment. As with so many similar cases no one will really ever know.

The only fatal, or for that matter, serious, accident involving the eight Mk 3 aircraft supplied to the SAAF occurred on 8 August 1953 when No 1718 of No 35 Squadron SAAF crashed on the Steynskloof mountains while taking part in a joint British/South African 'CAPEX' exercise.

This aircraft struck high ground in severe weather conditions which included winds gusting to 80kt and icing down to 3,000ft. It was thought at one stage that it might have been taking a 'short cut' in order to keep up with the exercise requirements. Thirteen lives were lost and it took several days for ground parties to reach the scene where it was immediately established that there had been no survivors. It is sometimes, perhaps rather cruelly, said that Shackletons have taken more lives from amongst their own crews than from any real or potential enemies, but all statistics are relevant, and as someone once wisely said there are lies, damned lies and statistics.

(Author's special note to historians: *An error in the recording of crashes occurred during the printing and publication of* Avro Shackleton *for which I take some responsibility. The details of two crashes were 'telescoped'. As the above list shows all eight on board were killed when Mk 3 XF704 of No 201 Squadron crashed into the Moray Firth on 8 December 1965. This aircraft was approaching Kinloss on a GCA let-down in bad visibility but no positive reason for the accident was proven. In* Avro Shackleton *this accident was confused with another two years later off Gan Island in the Indian Ocean in which eight aboard the aircraft were killed and three rescued.)*

8:

Prolonging the Shackleton's Active Life: Phase One

Above:
Gannet AEW3 XL502 is still being flown by the Fleet Air Arm's Memorial Flight, and is seen here over Mildenhall in May 1988. *Alan Curry*

The underlying reasons for the Shackleton's record-breaking longevity can logically be traced back to the Japanese attack on Pearl Harbor on 26 November 1941. Although the incoming raiders were in fact detected — by accident — on the screen of a ground-based radar station (the report from it being disregarded), complete surprise was achieved and an early outcome of the disaster was the launching of a crash programme in the United States under the codename 'Cadillac' for the provision of an AEW system.

In its broadest sense the phrase 'Airborne Early Warning' could be applied to any device which enables any admiral to 'see over the horizon' or any general to 'see over the hill'; even to the balloons and man-lifting kites of pre-World War 1 days. In the present context, however, the phrase really relates to the 'hoisting' of radar equipment to a height from which it can 'see' much further than any ground- or ship-based radar, and in particular see downwards on to low-flying enemy aircraft and missiles. In hindsight AEW seems to have been something of a Cinderella among the martial arts of this nation, although its importance has been magnified by many times since the end of World War 2.

Even if some of the past decisions do not fall into the blameworthiness category

(hindsight being the very fine thing that it is), a combination of what might be kindly called unfortunate errors of judgement has led to the curious position of Britain being dependent on what are literally museum-piece aircraft for one of its most vital defence tasks.

Beginning again from Pearl Harbor, the 'Cadillac' project resulted in the production of a radar set designated AN/APS20. By the end of the Pacific War the United States Navy was carrying sets of this type in carrier-based Grumman TBM3W Avengers, but there had scarcely been time for the crews to be worked up to battle efficiency before the war ended. As late as the spring of 1945 many US ships were sunk or damaged and some 5,000 lives lost from Kamikaze attacks during the final assault on Okinawa.

In postwar Britain little interest appeared to be taken in the development of AEW systems, certainly outside the Royal Navy which did acquire a fleet of Douglas AD4W Skyraiders supplied under the Mutual Defence Assistance programme in 1952. In spite of the nation's

early world lead in the invention of radar, the need for such a system to defend the mainland did not appear to be recognised and AEW remained very much a matter for the Navy. Fortunately this service continued to recognise its importance for the defence of its Fleets at sea and moved on to adopt the curious-looking but highly efficient Fairey Gannet AEW3 aircraft for the task. Forty-four of the Double Mamba Gannet 3s with their contra-rotating turbo-prop arrangement were built, each fitted with AN/APS20 radars of an improved mark with two control positions.

In the eye of the general public they tended to be the ugly ducklings of the Fleet Air Arm (almost literally because of their appearance) and when, in the late 1960s and early 1970s, arguments raged about the phasing out of the Navy's conventional fixed-wing aircraft carriers, most of these were about the loss of the strike and reconnaissance potential of the ships' Phantoms and Buccaneers rather than about the Gannets. As plans were made to phase out the last of the big carriers, HMS *Victorious*, *Eagle* and *Ark Royal*, the RAF

91

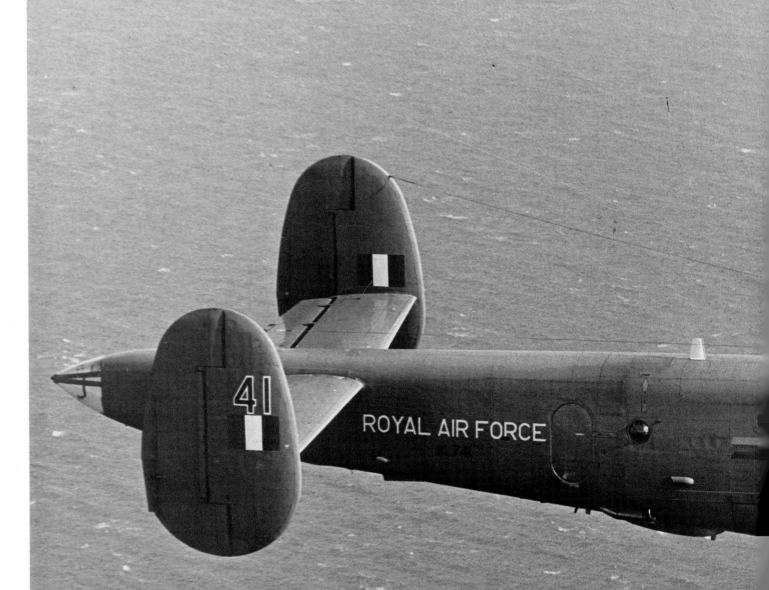

AEW2 WL741 of No 8 Squadron, Lossiemouth, going well. *BAe*

undertook to provide Airborne Early Warning for the Fleet, at least in northern waters. Its senior officers were by then confident that they would soon be provided with suitable, modern, land-based large aircraft to perform the task. Out of many projects two designs were in the immediate offing, the American Boeing E-3A Sentry carrying the Airborne Warning and Control System (AWACS) and a Nimrod variant. Numerous other designs existed on paper. Although the long controversy over the first two types was still to come, senior RAF officers were justifiably confident that they would get one or other within a few years, probably well before the planned date for the de-commissioning of the last conventional carrier, HMS *Ark Royal* in 1978.

The now often ridiculed phrase 'an interim solution' — referring to the temporary use of some spare Shackleton Mk 2s available because of the re-equipment of No 18 Group's MR squadrons with Nimrods — was at the time an entirely rational one. In the event, of course, no one really anticipated the 'interim solution' or 'temporary expedient' lasting nearly 20 years. The two phrases bring smiles in 1989 but in fairness they should not be held against those who coined them circa 1971.

Twelve Shackleton Mk 2s were selected for conversion to the 'temporary' AEW role. One reason for selecting Mk 2s rather than the later and more sophisticated Mk 3s was that the former had been subjected to less airframe fatigue, not having the Viper boosters fitted and having in general been flown under much lower all-up weights. The aircraft selected were: WL745, WL756, WL747, WR960, WR963, WL757, WL790, WL795, WL741, WL793, WR965 and WL754. The conversion work,

Above:
No 8 Squadron's badge.

Left:
After the de-commissioning of the last-but-one HMS *Ark Royal* — the last of the 'conventional' aircraft carriers — in 1978, the Navy lost its own AEW capability. The AEW2A version of the Sea King was hastily, but most effectively, improvised during the Falklands conflict but the aircraft arrived just too late to participate in the hostilities. A full squadron of this version of the versatile Sea King helicopters was later formed. Questions may be asked to the end of time whether some ships lost in the Falklands conflict might have been saved if more priority had been given to the whole subject of AEW within the Navy and the RAF. Again the only valid comment may be: 'Hindsight is a very fine thing'. Westland Helicopters Ltd

Below:
No 8 Squadron 'on parade' with their aircraft in 1983. RAF

which included partial re-sparring, was carried out at Hawker Siddeley's factory at Bitteswell, Leicestershire with the aircraft being finally assembled and test-flown from Woodford.

The main shape-change in the conversion was the fitting again of a chin-position radome to house the AN/APS20 scanner and the reappearance of the 'giant sparking plug' as part of the 'Orange Harvest' passive electronics countermeasures equipment which gives crews an indication that enemy radar signals are being aimed at them.

The first converted AEW2 flew at Woodford on 30 September 1971 with Jimmy Orrell again carrying out the air test. With a nice touch for history it was decided that the 'users' should be a re-formed No 8 Squadron RAF. This unit had a proud record going back to its formation on 1 January 1915 and a first war sortie on 28 April that year in a BE2C flown by Lts Holbrow and Murray RFC, reconnoitring for the Belgian Army. No 8 Squadron retained a distinguished record through World War 1 in the artillery observation role, but it is said (though by no means confirmed) that some of its officers incurred the displeasure of Lord Trenchard during an unrecorded jollification and that he decreed it should never serve in England again.

Be that as it may, No 8 Squadron went on to serve in the Middle East right up to and beyond Britain's departure from Aden in 1967 when it was flying Hunters, all that service contributing to the adoption of the Arabian 'Gambia' knife as a marking on its aircraft. With that sort of record No 8 Squadron was able to supply the rather special qualities of *élan*, *esprit de corps* and 'dash' required of a unit taking on a very challenging task which demanded a lot of

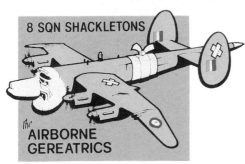

Above, top to bottom:

The 'Bear Hunters' badge, proudly displayed by No 8 Squadron and some others engaged in the deterrent task of nudging away Soviet intruders into UK air space.

One of many examples of No 8 Squadron's sense of humour. Somebody said, however, that 'the older you get the worse your spelling'.

This sticker has always appealed to the author. He has one on the bows of his sailing boat and sometimes wears a T-shirt with the same motif. Neither seem to work when it comes to dinghy racing at *his* age, however.

skill, a lot of hard work, and perhaps most importantly a sense of humour.

One of the first touches carried out on the squadron's re-formation on 1 January 1972 was the painting of its rather elitist fighter squadron markings on to the sides of its Shackletons. In their case they consisted of parallel red, blue and yellow stripes depicting, it is said, 'blood, sea and sand', from the Middle East days. The several talented artists within the squadron moved on to other things, producing the unofficial 'Bear Hunters' badge indicating that their main task was (and still is) the detection of Soviet reconnaissance aircraft intruding into British air space. Then they produced the slightly improper '8 Screws are Better Than Two Blow-Jobs' sticker referring to their sharing of RAF Lossiemouth with at least two fast-jet fighter squadrons, and the delightful 'Old Age and Treachery Will Triumph Over Youth and Skill' sticker, the latter still adorning the bows of the author's sailing dinghy even if the message does not often work these days.

Apart from the 'fun side' No 8 Squadron was presented with an enormous challenge on its re-formation with the former Fleet Air Arm station of Lossiemouth as a permanent base, while using nearby Kinloss temporarily until runway strengthening had been completed at the former airfield. It had, and still does have, to provide effective AEW cover for the UK Air Defence system over the critical Faroes Gap sea area between Iceland and Shetland, through which Soviet naval forces constantly travel, and over which Soviet aircraft endeavour to fly several days a week.

At a very early stage, therefore, a Quick Reaction Alert (QRA) system was evolved under which at least one Shackleton could be scrambled at a maximum of two hours' notice. This system which still obtains, and which will probably continue to obtain until at least 1991, involves a complete aircrew of nine being available for call-out either from on the station or from their homes, or nearby by bleeper, 24hr a day, seven days a week, 52 weeks a year. In addition it means a system under which groundcrews are available round the clock every day and night of the year with the special responsibility of beginning starting-up procedures on a large, complex — not to mention old — aircraft while aircrews are being assembled and briefed. The system bears all the hallmarks of Battle of Britain fighter squadrons on instant readiness and it has never failed.

(The author, residing in the home of an aircraft captain in April 1988, picked up the ringing telephone over breakfast at 09.10hrs one morning. A fellow guest was on 'Q Alert' — or just 'Q' to use squadron phraseology. He was legitimately still in pyjamas after a long training exercise the previous night. At 10.10hrs the author observed the 'Q' Shackleton taking off, fully manned, crew fully briefed, on its way to mark a suspect 'Bear' and then vector in some fighters to head it off.) It was just an

ordinary morning at No 8 Squadron, Lossiemouth.

On its re-formation in January 1972, No 8 Squadron was provided with the 12 converted Mk 2s listed above, and also for training purposes had the use of several other aircraft including WR967, the first Shackleton to reach the squadron. This aeroplane was damaged in a heavy landing at Kinloss in September of the same year. It was repaired — at the expenditure of 15,000 man-hours — but was later declared 'fatigue life expired' after a re-think by the stress engineers. Its fuselage was then converted at Lossiemouth into a radar crew simulator at a very economical figure, christened 'Dodo' after that famous extinct bird, and remains a very cost-effective form of equipment to this day, being regarded with much affection by all concerned.

The Gate Guardian at Lossiemouth (alongside a Gannet Mk 3) is WL738. It is something of a hybrid having been made to look like a Shackleton AEW2 with a chin radome but is somewhat shell-like inside. This aircraft served in No 8 Squadron as a trainer until October 1977. Several pieces, including some vital wiring harnesses were extracted from it circa 1985 for installation into the remaining operational aircraft. (This is the sort of equipment which, while probably procurable, would cost a great deal to make as a one-off item from new.)

Numbers WL801, WG556, WL787, and WG556 were also used by No 8 Squadron in its early AEW days and later scrapped.

With the 12 frontline aircraft originally provided, No 8 Squadron was able to provide highly effective AEW cover for the nation as well as offering training facilities for the RAF and other NATO air forces. It provided aeroplanes for displays around the country where the shape, and above all the sound, of something like a Lancaster was always much appreciated. 'No 8' also developed into an exceptional squadron of the RAF in that it retained its own first and second line engineering facilities plus those of the Civilian Working Party under its own roof, and indeed 'owned' its aeroplanes instead of drawing requirements day by day from a centralised servicing unit as is the case in many operational squadrons. From the start, too, it carried out its own aircrew conversion-to-type training and to some extent its own groundcrew conversion training. All this made for a special sort of spirit, then as now, much envied in other parts of the Service.

In the re-formed squadron's early days a major contribution was made by Fleet Air Arm observer officers from the Gannets who were able to pass on their vast knowledge of operating the AN/APS20 radars. Many served on attachment to the RAF in the middle 1970s, flying as 'back-enders' in the Shackletons.

In March 1977 a decision was announced by Mr Fred Mulley, Secretary of State for Defence in the Labour Government of the time, that Britain was going to buy the projected AEW3 version of the Nimrod in

preference to the Boeing E-3A AWACS Sentry or other alternatives on offer. His announcement was made after there had been a lot of prevarication over the adoption of a standardised NATO AEW system. After six years of multi-national argument the Government of the day came down with some justification in favour of what should have been an all-British system. In essence the idea was that Britain would produce and fly its own AEW aircraft but of course make them available to NATO — which in the end settled on the Boeing AWACS system.

The argument at the time, particularly when considered in the light of employment opportunities, seemed absolutely sound but even then the decision was viewed with some mixed feelings within the RAF in general and perhaps within No 8 Squadron in particular. Some of these mixed feelings were perhaps to do with professional airmen's liking for proven, rather than paper, designs; perhaps to do with the fact that for many, many years the RAF has happily flown and operated American-designed and built aircraft. By this stage No 8 Squadron had evolved a finely-honed system for the achievement of its task. The three components of the AEW task have been defined as 'Search, Find and Direct'; the last word used in contrast to 'Destroy' meaning that others have to complete the task of the destruction of an enemy, certainly not the lumbering old airborne radar station, be it based on the airframe of a beefed-up Lancaster, a Boeing AWACS or a Nimrod 3.

The AEW Shackletons therefore began a system of flying 'barrier patrols' over the Faroes Gap and over the northern half of the North Sea, the two areas over and through which the potential enemy might make forays. Initially an AEW aircraft carries out its 'Searching' and 'Finding' tasks, using its radar to look over the horizon and very importantly to look down on fast low-flying objects which in peacetime have to be distinguished from ships, civil aircraft and helicopters going about their legitimate business. Next it carries out its 'Direct' task, meaning that it becomes an airborne Fighter Control Unit vectoring much more lethal aircraft towards the intruders it has spotted. In recent years the second phase of the AEW task has been accorded increased recognition, including the introduction of a new aircrew half-wing brevet bearing the letters 'FC' (Fighter Controller) to date only worn by members of No 8 Squadron.

Operational sorties are normally flown at heights of about 5,000ft and last up to nine hours. These would be regarded as 'cushy' by old Shackleton hands with their memories of 18hr NAVEXES and 15,000ft altitudes, but are nevertheless demanding. This is particularly so on the 'back-end' crews who are working eyeball-and-chinagraph pencil radar sets in a still noisy, draughty, unpressurised aeroplane and during winter months obliged to wear survival 'goon suits' which make even climbing over the spar tunnels a hefty physical exercise.

Among its longevity claims the Shackleton is probably the last aircraft (perhaps apart from the Chipmunk) in RAF service to be equipped with ripcord parachutes as a means of escape in an ultimate crisis. A recent OC of No 8 Squadron did recommend that they could be removed to make some more badly needed space, but RAF policy decreed that they should remain.

In 1981 a devastating blow was delivered to No 8 Squadron by the Conservative Government's Defence Secretary, Mr John Nott, who announced that the aircraft strength was to be reduced from 12 to six — on grounds of 'economy'. This resulted in yet another unofficial No 8 Squadron sticker badge, this time declaring 'Join Shackair and get Notted'. Again perhaps the phrase 'hindsight is a very fine thing' could be quoted. In fairness to Mr Nott and the Government of the day there was every reason to believe that the AEW Nimrods would soon come into service. Whatever the rights or wrongs of the political decision, No 8 Squadron just got on with the job of providing AEW cover for the nation with six aeroplanes. For the next six years No 8 Squadron's engineers managed on average to produce four aircraft on the line by 09.00hrs most mornings, thus meeting the requirement for at least one available for a 'Q' Scramble and others for the heavy training commitments. A good record by anybody's standards in war or peace.

The aircraft retained by the squadron after the 'Nott Cut' were Nos WL756, WL747, WL963, WL757, WL790 and WR965. Under a rather jolly arrangement the original 12 Shackletons of No 8 Squadron were given the names of characters from the children's television series *Magic Roundabout* and *The Herbs*. Thus WL745 was 'Sage', WL756 'Mr Rusty', WL747 'Florence', WR960 'Dougal', WR963 'Parsley', WL757 'Brian', WL790 'Mr MacHenry', WL795 'Rosalie', WL741 'PC Knapweed', WL793 'Ermintrude', WR965 'Dill' and WL754 'Paul'. A subsequent OC of the squadron disapproved of this policy on the grounds that some very important aircraft should not be regarded as jokes, particularly within the RAF, and the names were removed. (However, WR960 now residing in the Air & Space Gallery of the Manchester Museum of Science and Industry has had its 'Dougal' name and symbol restored.)

Perhaps the saddest, most stupid, unfortunate and inefficient outcome of the 'Nott Cut' and the way it was handled was that six perfectly good aeroplanes which could have been serving the nation well at the time of writing this book were either burned, or turned into partly usable scrap. The best outcome was the retention of one of them (WR960 'Dougal') as a valuable museum exhibit and another (WL795) preserved as Gate Guardian at St Mawgan.

WL741 which entered service as a MR2 with No 224 Squadron in 1953 was last flown from Lossiemouth to Manston on 29 May 1981 for fire training. Although some components were recovered and returned to No 8 Squadron for spares, the rest of this aircraft was burned and scrapped.

WL745 which entered service in 1953 was flown as a Mk 2 by Nos 220, 42, 120, 204 and 205 Squadrons, and was in fact the AEW2 conversion prototype, last flew on 13 June 1981 from Lossiemouth to Catterick for fire training. Its last remnants had been burned by August 1982.

WL754 which entered service with No 37 Squadron in 1953 last flew from Lossiemouth to Valley on 22 January 1981. A valiant effort was made in the Anglesey area to raise funds for its preservation as an open air museum exhibit but this failed and the airframe was scrapped.

WL793, which entered service in 1953 and was flown by Nos 38, 204 and 210 Squadrons, was moved from the No 8

Squadron location at Lossiemouth to the fire dump in May 1981. It was partially burned for fire training and its remnants finally scrapped by bulldozer in July 1982.

WL795 which entered service in 1954 and was flown by Nos 204, 269, 210, 38 and 205 Squadrons, last flew from Lossiemouth to St Mawgan on 24 November 1981 for dumping but was 'rescued' as Gate Guardian.

WR960 which entered service in 1954 and was flown by Nos 226, 42, 210 and 205 Squadrons, also by 'B' Squadron A&AEE, last flew to Cosford from Lossiemouth on 22 November 1982 where it was dismantled and delivered to the Manchester Air & Space Museum for reassembly on 27 January 1983. (For further details of this aircraft's 'museum career' see later chapter.)

Even the relatively circumscribed flying involved in the AEW task can, of course, produce its 'hairy' moments, perhaps most frequently during exercises with other air forces in hostile climates. One such concerned (and the word is used advisedly) the crew of WL756, captained by Sqn Ldr (navigator) J. A. 'Jerry' Lane in August 1983 during an exercise based on Bodo in Norway. They encountered a rare succession of engine problems in appalling weather conditions, sent out a 'PAN' (Urgency) signal, fairly rapidly succeeded by a 'MAYDAY' (Distress) one. They had to overshoot on their first landing attempt at Bodo and divert to Andoya where they finally settled with a Norwegian S&R Sea King in close attendance.

An offer to the Andoya Air Traffic Controller to shut down what was left of their engines while they were still on the main runway was 'gratefully accepted'. When the crew left the aircraft, No 1 engine was so hot that there was a severe fire hazard and the area had to be cleared with a fire truck in attendance for 45min until it cooled down.

Jerry Lane and his crew all uttered those 'Phew-w-w-w' noises several times. Engineers from Lossiemouth eventually arrived to change all four engines on WL756 before it could be flown off again.

(Perhaps Bodo has some sort of spook for Shackleton crews. This event might be compared with the experience related by Allan Richardson earlier in this book referring to an event some 30 years earlier.)

During the period between the 'Nott Cut' and the final decision over the Nimrod AEW3 and the Boeing AWACS, members of No 8 Squadron went on displaying much resourcefulness, dedication and above all a sense of humour, but the last was beginning to wear thin by 1986 with no final decision made. Everyone from the OC to the newest posted technician had a sense of uncertainty, some of this related to his professional career, much of it to domestic arrangements.

Were the AEW Nimrods going to work and be accepted and when? Would they be required to stay at Lossiemouth and if so for how long? Would they be required to move to Waddington where the Nimrods were going to be based, and if so when? Should families be moved up to this fairly remote, if in many ways delectable, part of Scotland and children settled in local schools? Would it be better, especially for the sake of children of school age, for family separations to continue? All very human factors which seemed to be of little concern to those in high places still assessing the Nimrod 3's capabilities.

So it was perhaps with a sense of relief that most members of the squadron learned in December 1986 that a final decision had been made to abandon the Nimrod AEW project, albeit at a cost of close on £1 billion. Whatever the respective merits of the two types, No 8 Squadron had an 'end date' to plan on.

Left:
WL754 at its last resting place at Valley, photographed in 1985. *Alan Curry*

Below left:
WL795 at St Mawgan, destined for disposal but rescued as a Gate Guardian. *David Underhay*

Below:
Nimrod AEW3 XV 263 at Finningley in 1987. *Alan Curry*

9

Prolonging the Shackleton's Active Life: Phase Two

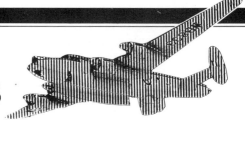

With the Boeing Sentries (AWACS) no longer available off the shelf the final rejection of the Nimrod 3 programme meant that the end-date for No 8 Squadron's Shackletons would be the early 1990s at best, meaning *another* four years of frontline operational service for them. This meant that though uncertainty had been removed, a great many other problems were being set for No 8 Squadron, especially for its fairly long-suffering engineers.

One of the first considerations which had to be faced was that a further programme of major overhauls would have to be instituted, the previous one having been concluded when it was thought that the aircraft would not be flying operationally beyond 1987 or 1988 at latest. The major overhaul problem was in fact solved remarkably expeditiously. The first Shackleton due for another 'major', WL756, was dealt with by RAF technicians from the Nimrod Major Servicing Unit at nearby Kinloss.

The work started on 2 September 1985 and was completed on 17 April 1986 with a total of 10,936 man-hours consumed. The total hours were in fact broken down to 1,524hr on scheduled servicing and 9,412hr on rectification and structural integrity work. Soon after, a very favourably priced tender by Airwork Ltd was accepted and the other five aircraft were all 'majored' by January 1988. The Airwork technicians were able to follow many of the schedules set up by the RAF team during the work on WL756.

The 'hours situation' on No 8 Squadron's remaining six Shackletons is worthy of record and study.

The table below shows in the first column the hours recorded when the aircraft were converted from MR2s to AEW2s at Bitteswell in 1971 and 1972. The second column shows their hours on 6 May 1988 after the last majors had been completed.

Aircraft	Hours at Conversion	Hours at 6/5/88
WL747	7,265	13,689
WL756	7,371	13,350
WL757	7,689	13,520
WL790	7,150	13,618
WR963	8,128	14,561
WR965	7,921	14,372

The Airwork team consisted of 25 technicians, many of whom were ex-RAF and Fleet Air Arm living in the Lossiemouth area, some with experience on Shackletons. Each aircraft took approximately 18 weeks to 'major' and the contract was only one week behind the promised date on completion. On top of all this it was clear to all concerned that the fatigue testing work which had been carried out for several years by the Civilian Working Party (CWP) from British Aerospace, the Design Authority would have to continue or indeed be stepped up.

This work was going on in a very big way at the time of writing in 1988, usually with two out of the squadron's six aircraft in the hangar with special attention being paid to the upper spar booms, the *most* special attention being to the inboard sections immediately above the undercarriage mountings. During the AEW conversion at Bitteswell in the early 1970s the lower sections of the main spars (the lower spar booms) had been completely replaced but not, for some reason, the upper booms.

Below:
A NATO AWACS Boeing E-3 Sentry at Alconbury in July 1985. *Alan Curry*

Above:
Looking at that critical top boom of the main spar of an AEW2 Shackleton of No 8 Squadron at Lossiemouth in 1988. Stephen Benn of the British Aerospace Civilian Working Party (BAe CWP) carrying out non-destructive testing with much care. *SAC Phil Regan RAF Lossiemouth*

The British Aerospace CWP technicians, many of whom have lived permanently in the Lossiemouth area and who regard themselves as very much a part of No 8 Squadron, were in 1988 using the latest in the way of non-destructive testing equipment, looking very closely at elongated (or 'ovalled') bolt-holes and strengthening where necessary. It became clear to any visitor to the squadron circa 1988 that no effort was being spared to ensure that the last of the Shackletons would fly *safely* until that end-date.

Another challenge facing the squadron was that the 'in-house training' would have to be continued. An arrangement to disband the Training Flight on the expectation that the Nimrods would be delivered by 1988 had to be abandoned and three more Aircrew Courses, Nos 38 and 39 were set up for 1988, with No 40 due to take place in 1989. Such courses, each designed to produce complete aircrews, are comprehensive. The conversion to type of young pilots who have gone through the standard RAF system of the 1980s, starting on Jet Provosts and moving on to Jetstreams if destined to go multi-engined, often poses some very intriguing problems.

The Shackleton is, apart from the Chipmunk, the last 'trail-dragger' in RAF service — certainly the only heavy one. A lot of instinctive adjustments therefore have to be made by and taught to, young pilots who have come up the Jet Provost-Jetstream route. To a squadron QFI it can be disconcerting if the first instinct is to push the yoke *forward* when the main wheels impact with the runway. Even old hands admit that the Shackleton is 'a bit of a handful' to put down gently, especially in cross-winds, let alone asymmetrically. With only six aeroplanes left and the main stresses on the spars coming up through the undercarriage legs the sort of 'bouncers' which wartime Lancaster pilots got away with cannot really be permitted too often on No 8 Squadron. In very simple terms just one classified 'heavy landing' requiring the appropriate inspection and checks could significantly reduce the nation's AEW capability during an ordinary week at Lossiemouth.

One expedient which was used to solve the instinct problems of a newly-posted pilot, was to arrange for him to do some hours in a Chipmunk of an Air Training Corps Air Experience Flight. It worked and he progressed rapidly. Now the squadron has a Chipmunk on strength for this very purpose. By the time this book appears something like 500 pilots and mission crews will have been converted to type within No 8 Squadron's own training resources.

The normal crew for an AEW Shackleton consists of nine — two pilots, a flight engineer, a navigator and five radar operators. Of these the flight engineer is usually a senior NCO or Warrant Officer (Master); some of the radar operators can be senior NCO or Master Air Electronics Operators, or equally commissioned Air Electronics Officers. Since 1981 the arrangement has been for the radar crew to be headed by a Tactical Co-ordinator (TACO). Under him is an Intercept Controller and three radar operators.

An important feature of the crewing is that the aircraft captain can often be the navigator rather than necessarily the first pilot. Two aircraft captains on No 8 Squadron at the time of writing were navigators. A previous squadron OC (Wg Cdr Cooper) was a navigator. This arrangement under which the aircraft captain is not necessarily the first pilot has of course been shared with the Nimrod MR squadrons for many years. It is an intriguing one from the 'command and control' point of view. History records that in the German Air Force of World War 1 the pilots of two-seater observation aircraft were often corporals, functioning as 'chauffeurs' with the observers very much the senior officers.

Something of the sort obtains in the Fleet Air Arm's anti-submarine warfare helicopters in which the observer (a commissioned officer) takes over tactical control once battle is joined. Again as history records there were some complicated situations in RAF heavy bombers during World War 2 where the pilot might be a sergeant, his navigator a commissioned officer. The arrangement in the Army Air Corps in which helicopter pilots are often sergeants or warrant officers is sometimes criticised by the other two Services on the grounds that a passenger — possibly a General — might 'pull rank' on a pilot during a crisis.

One can only say that the arrangement in No 8 Squadron, where the aircrews are a happy mix of commissioned, warrant and non-commissioned officers, seems to work without any sort of friction. Sqn Ldr 'Jerry' Lane, a navigator captain with his 10,000hr recently completed, said: 'It has always worked. Of course I don't tell the pilots

"COMRADE SIGNALLER - ASK THEM IF THEY ARE SERIOUS - OR IF THEY ARE MAKING ANOTHER FILM FOR THE B.B.C."

how to take-off or land or actually handle the aircraft, but they know I am the boss as far as all the tactical situations are concerned.'

By and large, then, the squadron's commitments since the Nimrod cancellation have been heavy by anyone's standards. The necessity for the extra round of major servicings, plus the scheduled and unscheduled servicing, has meant that since 1986 the squadron has not been able to call upon all its six aircraft at any one time. On top of the 'in-house' conversion training, five operational crews have had to be kept current on hours. One aircraft has always had to be available on

Below:
One of No 8 Squadron's Shackletons undergoing stress investigation by the BAe CWP at Lossiemouth in April 1988. *SAC Phil Regan RAF Lossiemouth*

'GOING TO HAVE TROUBLE SHADOWING THIS ONE - ITS TOP SPEED IS HIGHER THAN OURS!'   *E.S HOSKINS*   APRIL 1984

routine of AEW barrier patrols over the North Sea and the Faroes Gap, they have meant much hard work for all concerned. This is particularly so for the groundcrews who have frequently had to improvise during such matters as necessary engine and wheel changes.

When the announcement was made, along with the Nimrod/AWACS decision, that the Shackletons would have to go on flying for another four years, there was some head-wagging about probable spares problems. Although these have undoubtedly existed they have not been as alarming as many pundits forecast. In the event the key people such as Sqn Ldr Mike Duiguid the Senior Engineering Officer, Warrant Officer Peter Heap, and CTech Paul Emery have had to contend with 'patchy' problems often concerning minor (though nonetheless vital) items such as oxygen tubes, brake 'sacs' and seat covers, rather than major ones such as engines or wing sections.

In mid-1988 it was estimated that there were still a good number of Griffon engines available in the country, with the splendid back-up of Rolls-Royce at East Kilbride still available. Nevertheless some of the older ones have had to be nursed and cherished by such experts as CTech Mike Geach. As much care has to be taken over the vital translation units which took a lot of perfecting when the idea of contra-rotating propellers was first evolved circa 1944, and which are among a Shackleton's main means of support in the air.

QRA standby. There has also been a constant demand for Shackletons to appear at air displays and the like, and the number of curious visitors to the squadron has sometimes been almost embarrassing, though none have ever been turned away.

A special ingredient in the squadron training programme has been the sending of detachments usually of one aircraft and about 15 groundcrew, to Cyprus to work with RAF fighter squadrons at the Armament Practice Camp there. Other detachments have been visiting France to work with fighters of both L'Armée de L'Air and Aéronavale. While these detachments have provided welcome breaks from the

Below:
'The Boss' of No 8 Squadron in 1988, Wg Cdr David Hencken (left) and Flt Lt Roger Read, both Squadron QFIs. The aircraft is the beloved '747'. *Mike Arron,* Daily Telegraph

In 1987 there was a problem over the supply of main landing wheel tyres, probably the biggest of their kind still in use anywhere in the world, going at 64in outside diameter and 26in width. Dunlop then undertook to produce some more as rather expensive short-run items. (With 85lb/sq in in them the Shackleton tyres do allow for operations from grass, certainly for taxying around obstructions on per-

Above:
At the sharp end of '747': from left to right, Flt Lt Roger Read, Flt Lt Rupert Hornby and Wg Cdr David Hencken. *Mike Arron,* Daily Telegraph

Below:
The Battle of Britain Memorial Flight's Chipmunk 'greasing in' for a three-pointer.
Peter R. March

Above right:
A Shackleton of No 8 Squadron exercising with a Tornado F3 of No 29 Squadron.
RAF Lossiemouth

imeter tracks.) One bonus for the squadron engineers was the move from Cosford of Shackleton MR2 WL798, which had been flown by Nos 38, 205 and 204 Squadrons before grounding and allocation to No 2 School of Technical Training, mainly for the instruction of RAF apprentices on hydraulic systems. WL798 was brought by road to Lossiemouth in February 1987 and made available for cannibalisation with some special interest being taken in its wing sections. By mid-1988 its outer wing sections had been removed and some consideration being given to the inner sections as possible spares. (At one stage, circa 1984, the outer wing sections of WR960 in the Manchester Air & Space Museum were 'looked at' in case some sort of exchange deal might have been worthwhile. Perhaps, happily, this project did not proceed otherwise there might have been some even ruder remarks than those current at the time in the Shackleton's birthplace about the RAF wanting their museum exhibit back to fly again.)

On the general strength and longevity of the Shackleton airframes, Mr W. G. Heath, now Chief Structural Engineer at BAe, Woodford, recalls that when he was working on the design in the 1940s he had a gentle altercation with Mr Roy Chadwick about the dimensions of the spars he was proposing. Mr Heath told 'the great man' that for the sort of work the aeroplane would have to do the spar should be able to withstand a 2½g pullout. According to Mr Heath, in an article written for the Royal Aeronautical Society, Roy Chadwick replied: 'Two-and-a-half G! They mustn't do that with our aeroplane.' On later reflection Mr Heath thinks that he was having his leg pulled. Certainly the bigger spars were accepted.

The Shackleton's wing was also the first to be given a full-scale fatigue test in Manchester, Mr Heath recalls. The test took place at Chadderton in 1958 and revealed the shortcomings of several features. One of these was the attachment of the wing skins to the spars. Mr Heath's paper went on to record that the spar booms of the whole Lancaster 'family' were massive extrusions, roughly square in basic section but hollowed out to reduce weight wherever possible. The webs were attached by long bolts passing through the booms, thus necessitating a simple skin attachment if too much cross-sectional area was not to be lost:

'The Manchester and Lancaster had rivets driven into blind tapped holes. These were quite effective but difficult to remove for repair work. Later aircraft, including the Shackleton, used self-tapping screws.

'Since the pitch and depth of the holes for these screws was not closely controlled, there was an occasional (and random) breakthrough into the web attachment bolt

Tyres CAN be a problem, even unto themselves.
Artist unknown

"ONCE MORE, THATS ALL, JUST ONCE ※!※/※ MORE !"

Above:
New propeller blades are still available from British Aerospace at Lostock, near Bolton — formerly de Havilland Propellers — but thay have to be fitted with much care into the critical translation unit of a Griffon contra-rotator. Cpl Rikingram and J Tech Muir of No 8 Squadron carrying out this very important task. *SAC Phil Regan RAF Lossiemouth*

Below:
Mr Harry S. Gartsman.

holes. This intersection provided an ideal location for the start of a fatigue crack.

'The discovery of the precise locations of all such breakthroughs across the fleet, and the sebsequent cleaning out of the junction to remove the stress-raiser has occupied many hours on the non-destructive test team from the Manchester Structures Department.'

(Author's note: *Mr Heath's comments made in 1984 are reproduced at some length because they give an idea of the importance of the engineering tasks still being carried out at Lossiemouth, both by No 8 Squadron engineers and the BAe CWP.*)

Another very big bonus came to No 8 Squadron, in particular to its avionics specialists, in the 1980s when a long-standing relationship between various British purchasing missions in Washington and the firm of Alvaradio Industries Inc, associated with Hasgar Industries at no less an address than Sunset Boulevard, Beverly Hills, bore fruit in the form of a number of unused AN/APS20 radars being made available to the RAF at a very modest cost. The founder of this American company, Chicago-born Mr Harry S. Gartsman, now aged 72, is an Anglophile who still retains close personal relationships with the RAF in general and with No 8 Squadron in particular, although he officially retired from business in 1981 and handed his company over to his son-in-law, his chief engineer and his general manager.

In the mid-1980s No 8 Squadron received 18 still crated AN/APS20 radars which, after a very little 'drying out' on removal from their packing cases, worked

perfectly. Mr Gartsman's organisation, via other close relationships with GEC, has also been able to assure the squadron of a continued back-up of spares, some of them held in stock, others made from drawings and licences which his former company still hold.

Mr Gartsman appears to have been one of many who foresaw the Nimrod 3 problems, even from the other side of the Atlantic, and he takes an intense pride in the help he has been able to give to the RAF. This 'bonus' came in the nick of time. By the mid-1980s the original AN/APS20s from the Fleet Air Arm Gannets were showing signs of sheer old age with the 'pictures' looking a bit like those from aged black-and-white TV sets.

Many of the RAF's best technicians welcome a posting to No 8 Squadron because it provides opportunities for 'real engineering', and the challenges of impro- visation as opposed to circumscribed

Above:
WL757 going well in 1988 . . .

Overleaf:
. . . and WL793 going well, too.
RAF Lossiemouth

'box-changing' in the high technology squadrons and establishments. Others enjoy the location, perhaps, because of the beauty of the Morayshire and Speyside surroundings and the opportunities for all sorts of outdoor activities at relatively low cost. Others are less happy because they feel the work may be taking them out of the mainstream of their careers. Some dislike the remoteness of the station and the travelling time and cost involved in keeping in touch with families and friends in the South. Rather similar attitudes apply

among newly-posted aircrews. However, visitors to No 8 Squadron — and there are many of them — invariably come away feeling that this is a very exceptional unit of the nation's armed forces, with a very special form of morale.

At the time of writing the squadron was planning a special event for the 8th day of August which, of course, was going to be '8-8-88' in official terminology. Invitations were sent to every 'No 8 Squadron' in NATO and in some other friendly air forces.

A sight which particularly gladdened the eyes of No 8 Squadron's SENGO (Senior Engineering Officer) and his staff, and also those of the BACWP at Lossiemouth — four of the last six AEW2s in formation to mark the momentous date of '8-8-88' *RAF Lossiemouth*

10

Preserving the Memories

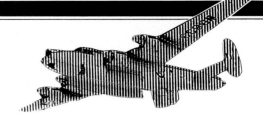

One of many good reasons for writing this book was that something of a Shackleton cult was emerging in the aviation world as the type approached the 40th anniversary of its first flight. As a lay author I may not be fully qualified to judge, but I find it hard to think of any other aircraft type which has engendered so much affection amongst those who have flown it, continue to fly it, and amongst those who helped to design and build it, and to maintain it from the ground.

Counterarguments to that assertion may of course be put up by those with affectionate memories of Spitfires, Hurricanes, Dakotas, Rapides and Tiger Moths, to name but a few; but there has always seemed to have been something 'special' about the regard for the Shackleton, displayed in the hundreds of communications I have received in the course of writing two books about this aeroplane.

There could be a number of reasons for this clearly demonstrated emotion about some bits of metal put together to form an aeroplane. '10,000 rivets' somebody once said; somebody else said '20,000 rivets' and so on. One reason for the emotion could be that those involved with the Shackleton have been, in the main, engaged in peacetime operations. Perhaps, therefore, their memories have not been clouded by the real horrors of war which have affected many of those who flew Lancasters, Spitfires and Hurricanes and all the other glamorous aeroplanes of World War 2.

A number of old Shackleton hands, and indeed old Lancaster aircrews, who have

Below:
Allan Richardson, former pilot in No 120 Squadron during its 1950s Acceptance Trials (right of picture) with the author looking at WR960 in the Manchester Museum in 1988. Allan Richardson's first comment on mounting the ladder was: 'My God, it still SMELLS the same.'
Mike McCabe

Right:
One of the first bits of WR960 to be brought through the doors of the Manchester Air & Space Museum, later restyled the Air & Space Gallery of the Manchester Museum of Science & Technology. *Alan Curry*

Below right:
Allan Richardson relives some memories during a visit to No 8 Squadron at Lossiemouth in the summer of 1988. *Mike McCabe*

climbed aboard Shackleton WR960 in the Manchester Museum have said in my presence: 'My God, it still SMELLS the same.' The sense of smell is perhaps the most evocative of all the senses when it comes down to memory of past events. It seems that there is something about the smell of WR960 and about that of the other museum-preserved Shackletons which triggers off memories. The interior smell of a Shackleton, and for that matter of a Lancaster, is supposed to be composed of a mixture of leaking high octane petrol, hydraulic fluid, oil, dirty leather from the aircrew seats, and — dare one mention it — exhudation from men's bodies under great stress.

To younger generations the Shackleton has the special attraction of being a still flying, and still operational example of the sort of aircraft which helped to win World War 2 and which gave to them the chance to live the sort of lives they now choose. In the author's opinion there are more young men and women of that sort of viewpoint than many others in the nation suspect. Therefore the preservation of the Shackle-

ton in some form should be regarded as a matter of long-term national importance. Taking a long-term view of aviation history, this nation is probably well served with non-flying museum Shackleton exhibits.

The location of the Shackleton bases may also have contributed to the creation of a special 'corporate feeling'; *esprit de corps*, general comradeship, or whatever one cares to call the essential motivation of any good Air Force, Army or Navy. Places like Ballykelly (with Aldergrove down the road) in Northern Ireland, Kinloss in Morayshire, and St Eval in Cornwall were remote places where the people living in them, including RAF people, tended to

huddle together and make their own mutual comforts, their own amusements, and thereby became special communities. The overseas Shackleton bases such as Aden, Sharjah, Masirah Island, Singapore, Labuan Island, and a bit later Majunga, were all places where airmen had to live on each other's resources and support one another, often through their own sense of humour. Out of all that, one feels, there has grown this special affection for an aeroplane type which has bonded so many together.

Another reason for the affection for the aircraft type on a wider base could be its resemblance to the immortal Lancaster, in shape and perhaps especially in sound.

Below:
WR960 reassembled and gleaming after much tender loving care by its restoration team in the Manchester Museum. *Alan Curry*

Right:
WR960 in the Manchester Air & Space Museum together with restorers and a No 8 Squadron aircrew in foreground. *Alan Russell*

Even though the Merlins of a Lancaster have been replaced by Griffons with contra-rotating propellers, the sound of a Shackleton overhead at an air display or somewhere still conjures up those words 'it sounds like one of ours'.

Much of the writing about World War 2 aeroplanes, and about World War 1 types such as the Sopwith Camel and the SE5A for that matter, has concentrated on the glamour, the excitement and the successes; and has perhaps rightly not dwelt all that much on the truly terrible aspects of flying in a war. Perhaps because of this most of the memories of old Shackleton hands are reasonably happy ones. By and large the Shackleton has 'flown at peace'.

Another good reason for the affection shown to this aeroplane type could be that so many men shared arduous experiences in it, both in the air and around it on the ground. There can probably be no closer-knit group of people than an aircrew.

Shackletons have always required, and continue to require, large aircrews ranging down from 13 at the peak of their MR responsibilities, to at least nine in their final AEW role. At one stage Shackleton aircrews were especially closely-knit because they were often 'all NCO'. (Commissioned officers should NOT take offence at this assertion. There is a very special bond between non-commissioned-officers in all three Services, and the author happens to know quite a lot about it in case any reader wants to argue.)

The curious situations in World War 2 where an aircraft captain could be a sergeant and his navigator a flying officer have been explored by many aviation writers. So far as this book is concerned it may only be necessary to record that a lot of Shackleton captains held such ranks as flight sergeant and distinguished themselves.

Pride of place in the list of Shackleton Museum exhibits must go to WR960, the AEW2, lovingly preserved, and still being updated by a voluntary team in what is now called the Air & Space Gallery of the Manchester Museum of Science and Industry. It is entirely right and proper that this should be so because Manchester was the birthplace of the Shackleton, the place where it was conceived in shape, if not in final precise design by Roy Chadwick. The place where all 190 (or were there 191?) Shackletons were built partly at Chadderton and finally assembled and flown just down the road at Woodford, which is technically in Cheshire, but which is part of what used to be called Greater Manchester. When all is said and done the Shackleton is a Manchester aeroplane.

WR960 came to Manchester's Air Museum by devious routes. At just about the time that the city of Manchester was contemplating the establishment of an aviation museum the 'Nott Cut' had taken its effect on No 8 Squadron at Lossiemouth. The RAF Museum at Hendon put in an immediate bid for one of the AEW2 Shackletons about to be made redundant. At about the same time the Hendon administrators discovered that they did not really have room for another large aircraft so they offered this Shackleton to Manchester.

So WR960 ('Dougal' in the temporary No 8 Squadron nomenclature) was flown from Lossiemouth to RAF Cosford on

Top:
Six of the restorers at the Manchester Museum. Note the proud wearing of groundcrew overalls with No 8 Squadron badges which they have been given official permission to wear. *Mike McCabe*

Above:
Close-up of the No 8 Squadron groundcrew badge, a little more than many 'Erks' of World War 2 days were ever entitled — or allowed — to wear. *David Underhay*

Right:
The Manchester Museum 'groundcrew' at work. *Mike McCabe*

22 November 1982. There it was dismantled and brought in many pieces by road and through the original doors of the Manchester Air & Space Museum. It was initially reassembled by a team of RAF technicians with some local help and advice and appeared as a whole aeroplane again in February 1983. Since then a hard-working and dedicated team of enthusiasts and restorers has put in close on 2,000 man-hours, not only to improve the exterior appearance of the aircraft but also to add and fit equipment to the interior, with the aim of achieving as much realism as possible for the thousands who pass through this outstanding aviation museum every year.

Piece by piece more cockpit instruments have been acquired, more sections of AN/APS20 radars obtained and fitted. By 1988 flying control cables had been obtained and fitted so that very privileged visitors could sit on the flight deck and operate the elevators and rudders — aileron controls were due to come later.

(On one evening in 1988, in the presence of the author, a former Shackleton pilot and a former air gunner of No 617 Squadron went and sat down together in the cockpit of '960'. About two-and-a-half hours later they were extracted with cries that the pub across the road would be shutting. The rudders of '960' had been seen to swing, the elevators rise and fall, but nobody dared ask these two where they had actually been in their imaginations.)

One of the main aims of the Manchester restoration team, headed by Mr Denis Stead, has been to add realism. While it has not been possible to make '960' a walkthrough exhibit without cutting a separate and unrealistic door on the port

Left and below left:
Air Training Corps cadets inside WR960 at the Manchester Museum. Compare the realism created with a 'live' crew shot taken by the author on board an AEW2 of No 8 Squadron

Top:
VP293 'Zebedee' at the Strathallan Museum in November 1980. *Alan Curry*

Above:
WR977 at the Newark Museum in 1986. *Alan Curry*

side of the fuselage, visitors are now able to walk up a ladder and look forward into the fuselage and see an almost exact reproduction of the radar and instrument layout of a Shackleton AEW2. A sound tape has been produced incorporating all the noises of a full engine start-up complete with the appropriate aircrew intercom chatter, plus some extracts from the chatter taking place on a typical training sortie.

With Manchester as the acknowledged home of the Shackleton there is also a plan afoot to deposit and preserve all the archive material about the type in the area, possibly at Manchester International Airport in charge of that distinguished aviation historian, Mr Brian Robinson. This is an important project since many of the early archives about the type were destroyed in a fire at the Chadderton Avro works many years ago.

At the time of writing, several other Shackletons were on view at museums and as Gate Guardians at RAF stations. They were:

VP293: originally built as a Mk 1, converted to a T4 trainer and christened 'Zebedee', perhaps because of its recorded habit of bouncing on landing. This aircraft is preserved at the Strathallan Museum in Scotland. It began its career as one of the first Shackletons delivered to No 236 OCU in 1951. It then served in No 224 Squadron at Gibraltar and with Nos 42 and 206 Squadrons at St Eval. On converstion to a T4 it served with the Maritime Operational Unit and later with the Weapons Flight at Farnborough.

WR977: a Mk 3, is on display at the privately-run Newark Air Museum. This aeroplane began its career in 1957 as a 'Phase One' with No 220 Squadron at

St Eval and No 201 Squadron at St Mawgan. It was upgraded to Phase Two in 1959 and issued to No 206 Squadron, St Mawgan, with the code letter 'B'. It was twice damaged in accidents then went to No 201 Squadron at Kinloss, coded 'O' in 1963. After further upgrading to Phase Three it went to No 42 Squadron coded 'B' in 1966, was modified to take the Viper jets

in 1968 and went to No 203 Squadron at Ballykelly again coded 'B'. It then also served with Nos 206 and 42 Squadrons, back to 203 at Luqa, Malta, and finally 'retired' in 1970, kept first at Thorney Island and then Finningley. In 1977 it was due to be scrapped to make room at Finningley for the Royal Review of the RAF but was bought by Newark Museum

member Mr Stuart Stevenson. It was dismantled and brought to Newark on seven lorries and re-assembled by museum members in four weeks.

XF708: a Mk 3, is housed at the Imperial War Museum at Duxford as a static exhibit and is much photographed by visitors to displays and open days there. XF708 went into service with No 201 Squadron in 1959 and No 120 Squadron in 1964. From 1968 to 1972 it served with No 203 Squadron first at Ballykelly and then in Malta. It was flown to Duxford in August 1972 by which time it had flown more than 6,500hr and made nearly 2,500 landings. By mid-1988 No 2 School of Technical Training at Cosford still held four Mk 3 Shackletons but they were 'up for disposal', meaning that they would probably be scrapped unless other museum buyers came forward, or some more places found for Gate Guardians. These aircraft, Nos WR971,

Above left:
XF708 at Duxford in 1988. *Alan Curry*

Left:
WL801 with crew prior to its delivery to Cosford. *RAF*

Top:
WR974 at Cosford in 1982. *Alan Curry*

Below:
South African Shackleton No 1716 at the November 1983 Air Africa International display at Lanseria Airport near Johannesburg. It gave a flying display on the final day, the last time a Mk 3 flew in public in the world. *Louis Vosloo*

985, 982 and 974 had been used for training technicians on hydraulics, control systems and other procedures. WR974 was in fact officially the property of the RAF Museum, Hendon. As related previously, Cosford handed over Mk 2 WL798, which had been used in a similar way, to No 8 Squadron at Lossiemouth in 1987 for cannibalisation in view of the further extension in Shackleton service. The Cosford Shackletons were to be replaced by more up-to-date 'grounded' aircraft of the jet age. The Gate Guardians already referred to are AEW2 WL795 at St Mawgan and the hybrid MR2 WL738 at Lossiemouth. There is a T4 nose section at the Helston Aero Park, near Culdrose in Cornwall.

By the end of 1988 the seven grounded South African Shackletons were disposed of as follows:

No 1716 was in open storage at the SAAF Museum, Swartkop, Pretoria and the engines were regularly run with a view to possible restoration to flying condition.

No 1717 was displayed at the Natal Parks Board Museum, Midmar Dam.

No 1720 (temporarily wrongly painted as 1719 due to an administrative complication) stood as Gate Guardian at the Ysterplaat Air Force Base.

No 1721 was also located at Swartkop in ground-running condition and had been earmarked for a possible exchange 'with foreign interests'.

No 1722 was hangared by No 35 Squadron at Swartkop with engines being occasionally ground-run. This aircraft was also earmarked for a possible exchange or sale.

No 1723 was mounted on the roof of 'Vic's Viking Garage' on the Johannesburg-Vereeniging road. It got there as the result of a triple deal under which the owner, an aviation enthusiast, handed over his Vickers Viking to the South African Airways Museum and the latter passed on a Ventura to the SAAF Museum!

No 1719 (the original aircraft of that number) was held by the University of Stellenbosch Flying Club in a partly dismantled condition. Prospects of restoration were questionable.

In mid-1989 plans were being evolved to 'rescue' Mk 3 No WR971 from RAF Cosford and put parts of it on display in the UK under the aegis of Wellesley Aviation with the possible support of the Shackleton Association.

(As recorded earlier **No 1718** was lost in a crash in August 1973.)

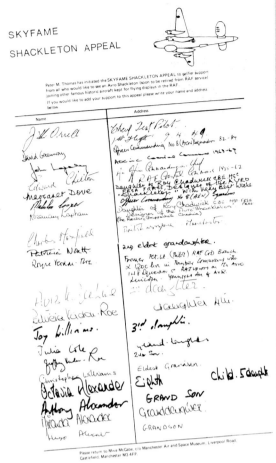

SKYFAME
SHACKLETON APPEAL

Peter M. Thomas has initiated the SKYFAME SHACKLETON APPEAL to gather support
from all who would like to see an Avro Shackleton (soon to be retired from RAF service)
joining other famous historic aircraft kept for flying displays in the RAF.
If you would like to add your support to this appeal please write your name and address
below.

Please return to Mike McCabe, c/o Manchester Air and Space Museum, Liverpool Road,
Castlefield, Manchester M3 4FP.

Above left:
Signatures on the appeal by Peter Thomas for funds to keep a Shackleton flying.

Above and right:
Jim Crail and crew with '747' in the 1950s (right). He took this picture (above) of his beloved '747' in July 1988. It had been arranged for him to fly in her again but a night QRA intervened. In spite of his disappointment Jim said he felt an intense sense of pride at seeing his old aircraft 'scramble' on an operational mission and return with mission accomplished, nearly 40 years on. *Jim Crail*

Below right:
An early Mk 2 and a Mk 1. The Mk 2 is the famous 'WL747'. *Barry Peach*

Curiously, in some ways the best hopes of a Shackleton being maintained in flying condition after 1991 seemed to lie in South Africa or one of the 'foreign interests' mentioned above. Nevertheless, in 1988 valiant efforts were still being made by Mr Peter Thomas of 'Skyfame' in Lairg, Sutherland, to raise support to preserve one of the RAF aircraft in flying condition. Mr Thomas, who secured the Sunderland on display at Hendon from the French Navy, had obtained more than 18,000 signatures to a petition urging this objective but clearly a very large sum of money indeed would be needed. He was seeking commercial sponsorship with his usual drive and energy.

At one stage it seemed that the retention of one aircraft might be justified for the training of future aircrews of the RAF's Battle of Britain Memorial Flight Lancaster. Even this possibility, however, seemed remote under the financial stringencies of the late 1980s. The Memorial Flight, whose remit really confines it to World War 2 aircraft, does hold a Devon for asymmetrical flying practice and, like No 8 Squadron, a Chipmunk for 'tail-dragger' three-point landing technique polishing. No 8 Squadron was expected to continue to offer occasional training facilities for the Memorial Flight until the 1991 end-date.

A further possibility might of course be the arrangement of some sort of deal with the 'Republican Air Force' but this was being regarded as very much a last resort by the preservationists since it would presumably mean the aircraft being out of the UK for at least most of the time.

The 'cult' was much strengthened by the creation in 1987 of The Shackleton Association, curiously having its beginnings in Australia under the initiative of John Botwood who has made an important contribution to this book. There seemed to be some difficulties over arranging the administration of the Association in the UK during 1988 but, nevertheless, it appeared to be going from strength to strength to judge from the contents of its always well-produced and entertaining newsletters.

The author took considerable pride in being made a founder member, probably the only colour-blind ex-journalist, ex-soldier they will ever have. The 'putting in touch' of old friends is always an enjoyable and rewarding experience. In some cases old Shackleton hands have not only been put in touch with their old friends, but have also been put in touch with their old aeroplanes!

In 1986 Mr Jim Crail of Basingstoke wrote to the author, having spotted the airframe number WL747 as being one of those still operated by No 8 Squadron. Jim had flown this aeroplane as a MR2 in the 1950s, his first flight in her being in August 1953, and a 'reunion' after 34 years was duly arranged at Lossiemouth.

A little later another link-up was arranged between Jim Crail and Barry Peach of Chesterfield who had copies of a painting showing '747' flying as a Mk 2 of No 269 Squadron at Ballykelly in company with a Mk 1. Shackleton WL747, named 'Florence' in the period when No 8 Squadron named its aeroplanes after characters in the children's TV serial, will probably always have a special place in many memories. In 1988 it was rated as the best, the smoothest and the fastest of the last six being flown by No 8 Squadron, and all other things being equal it was usually the one 'the Boss' (Wg Cdr David Hencken) chose to fly. It was often the one that No 8 Squadron chose to send to air displays. Many concerned in the preservation of Shackletons have a special

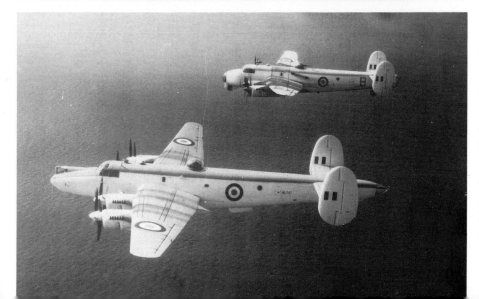

affection for '747', for a number of individual reasons.

On 9 March 1989 No 8 Squadron brought five out of the last six flying Shackletons down to Woodford from Lossiemouth to mark the 40th anniversary of the type's first flight from this airfield.

It was an impressive occasion with four out of the five aircraft doing low-level flypasts, first in box formation, then in line astern, with about 100 invited guests watching plus most of the 3,500 workforce at the BAe factory still prospering at Woodford. The landing of the five aircraft in a 30kt wind at about 45° across the only long runway at Woodford was particularly impressive. The sight of it warmed many an old airman's heart and would undoubtedly have warmed that of Jimmy Orrell if he had lived to see the day.

A good time was had by all a little later at the Air & Space Gallery of the Greater Machester Museum of Science and Technology, part of it alongside WR960. At this event it was officially announced that No 8 Squadron will fly the AWACS from Waddington, England, when they come into service in 1991 in spite of the legendary tale that the Squadron had incurred the displeasure of Lord Trenchard circa 1918 and that he had decreed that it should never again serve in England. (The Squadron, as recorded, then spent a lot of time in the Middle East and eventually in a country called Scotland!) The Shackleton Association also held its first reunion in Manchester on 4 March 1989, as near as they could get it to the 'The Shack's' 40th Birthday.

11:

Plans for the Final Succession

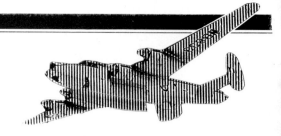

By mid-1988 the RAF was able to indicate its plans for the eventual takeover of the AEW responsibility from the Shackletons of No 8 Squadron by the seven Boeing E-3s (AWACS) under order. It is intended that these aircraft will enter RAF service from a Main Operating Base at Waddington, Lincolnshire — the temporary 'home' of a number of the ill-fated Nimrod AEW3s, and where some of these still resided up to mid-1988, pending a decision on their disposal.

At the turn of the decade the RAF was about to establish its own training squadron for both air- and groundcrew at Waddington for what were going to be known as the 'RAF E-3s'. It was envisaged that the first conversion courses would start in late 1990 and that, thereafter, all air- and groundcrew training for these aircraft would take place at Waddington. In 1987 an agreement had been reached between the UK and the Member Nations of NATO which control the 'NE-3A Component' — that is the NATO AWACS — for one complete RAF crew to be trained on these aircraft. This first course completed its training by the spring of 1988 and was destined to remain at the NATO AWACS Force HQ at Geilenkirchen, West Germany, until sometime in 1990. Individual crew members have been totally integrated into the three operational squadrons of the NATO Force and fly regularly alongside crew members from other nations.

In 1988 it was also planned that the UK should send another 40 aircrews to Geilenkirchen to be trained with the NE-3A Component. It was expected that this training would be completed by mid-1990, whereupon all the UK crew members would return to Britain to form the cadre of the RAF E-3 Operational and Training Squadrons.

Also in 1988, technician groundcrews began training at Tinker Air Force Base, Oklahoma under a Foreign Military Sales Agreement with the USAF. On return to the UK they were destined to form the cadre of instructors for the RAF E-3 Maintenance Course.

By mid-1988 a total of 17 RAF officers had been attached to the NE-3A Component of NATO, thereby having gained much experience to 'pass down the line'.

By the time of the fateful decision against the Nimrod AEW3, NATO E-3s were regularly deploying to RAF Waddington to participate in exercises with RAF and Royal Navy units and this, of course, is continuing. USAF E-3s also occasionally deploy to the United Kingdom to take part in exercises. Other USAF E-3s working out of Iceland often operate in support of that nation's Defence Force and sometimes divert to airfields in the United Kingdom in bad weather conditions — these arrivals often forming the substance of 'spotters' reports and photographs.

By mid-1989, therefore, all seemed set fair for a smooth takeover of the nation's AEW coverage by the RAF E-3 Force from the faithful last six Shackletons of No 8 Squadron, just about the time of the latter aeroplane's completion of 40 years in RAF frontline service.

Right:
Members of the Shackleton Association gathered round WR960 in Manchester on 4 March 1989. *Tony Henn*

Below:
A USAF Boeing E-3B Sentry of the 963rd AWACS in flight. *USAF*